THE YES AND NO OF CONTEMPORARY ART

HARVARD UNIVERSITY PRESS · CAMBRIDGE · 1957

The Yes
and No
of
Contemporary Art

AN ARTIST'S EVALUATION

George Biddle

© Copyright, 1957, by the President and Fellows of Harvard College

Distributed in Great Britain by
Oxford University Press, London

Library of Congress Catalog Card Number 57–7606
Printed in the United States of America

To M. J. B.

*Who some day will add his own mite
to the heritage of American art*

ACKNOWLEDGMENTS

My grateful thanks are due to Van Wyck Brooks, Bernice Kenyon, Robert Beverly Hale, Edmund Nash and MacKinley Helm, who have helped me with their advice and criticism; and to the many artists, without whose friendship or inspiration these pages could not have been written.

G. B.

CONTENTS

ILLUSTRATIONS

The decoration on the title page is from a lithograph by the author expressing the motto, "Nor hatred, nor fear, nor ignorance shall ride our world." Death riding on a mad horse has been frequently used by the author, in his murals and also on his bookplate, to symbolize the unleashed forces of evil and destruction in the world today.

INTRODUCTION

Since I consider art as a means of communi-
cation as well as a vehicle for self-expression,
I have always desired that my work be known
to many people . . . The content of my art
is people — men, women and children, not in
isolated portraiture, but within their daily
setting . . . I choose to be a realist and hu-
manist in art. It is difficult to do this today in
this period of general confusion. There is an
encouraging trend, however, among many
artists all over the world — a groping to find a
way of return to basic human values.

— Raphael Soyer

Ma pensée retourne à son interrogation:
Est-ce là le crépuscule du soir, ou l'aurore?

— Andre Gide

I am always drawn toward Heaven; I
reach upward to Heaven. I was never the
painter or sculptor merely to do a shop job.

— Michelangelo

INTRODUCTION

From the Author's Tahitian Diary: Tupuai, South Pacific, April 20, 1922. Our ninety-foot schooner is loaded. In the hold some hundred tons of copra, and the cockpit, too, piled above the rudder-box with more bales of copra. In the cabins sacks of starch above the level of the upper bunks. The water tanks moved aft to clear the main deck. Here stalls have been set up and lashed together from purao *poles; and some twelve cows and forty pigs have been hoisted aboard. Up in the bow are two hundred chickens in crates. A dozen turkeys; a few made fast by the leg to the capstan; others wandering aimlessly about, in a state of ruffled and awkward dignity. Forward of the galley-house great piles of banana, golden* fei — *the mountain plantain — and fodder for the animals; and more* fei, *banana, breadfruit and baskets of oranges hung over the rail for the crew. Also thirty natives, bound from Tupuai to Rurutu.*

Before sitting down to our evening meal out on deck in the rain, there was a silence. The natives uncovered. One of them prayed.

"C'est bien le genre kanaque! — Just what you'd expect of the Kanakas," snarled the half-caste supercargo.

April 23, 1922. The Tuamotuan captain, crouched on the deck by the rudder, told story after story of the tau Tahiti, the ancient legendary days.

He told of the two children who sat at home, each with a slice of breadfruit in his hands, waiting for their parents, who had gone to spear fish by torchlight on the outer reef. The little ones waited and waited, but their parents lingered forgetful on the reef and ate the fish. At length the children grew tired of waiting and flew up into the sky. And there they remain unto this day, clinging together, Pipiri ma, the Pleiades. The parents call in vain: "Come back, come back!" But Pipiri ma are angry and will never more return. The legend has become a nursery rhyme which mothers sing to quiet their children.

> *"Pipiri ma*
> *Come back to us!"*
> *"We shall never return to you."*
> *Ill was the night fishing by torchlight.*

The children were disappointed in the catch.
They are changed into twin flower clusters,
Purple-flaming in the sky.

He told of his own grandfather, a tahua, a witch doctor from one of the islands of the Tuamotu, the Dangerous Archipelago. He would steal a bit of his enemy's hair and a thread or two from his loin cloth; and as he shook hands with the man, he would scratch off a little dirt from the palm of his hand. All this he would wrap together in the husk of a coconut along with a lizard. And with this he could bewitch and slay whom he would.

He told of the islander and his servant who were swallowed by a shark and carried to a distant atoll among the Tuamotu. Now in this atoll there were no men, and the women cohabited with sea-cucumbers. The islander prevailed on one of the women to sleep with him. She found him more congenial than a sea-cucumber and spoke to her companions. And eventually he and his servant had many children by the women of the island. But his servant's children were all born with wings; and they kept them hidden under a peue — a pandanus mat. One day the peue was removed and the children flew away; and no man has heard of them since. But the rest remained; and to this day their descendants live on the island. Even to this day — E teie mahana!

He told of the aito, the hero, who was so strong that he could cast a cliff from one lagoon to the other. He could piss a mile, a great waterspout, so that his enemies were drowned in the stream of his urine. He was so enormous that one day when he fell he broke the island in two. And so it has remained even to this day — E teie mahana!

Lastly, he told of the island in the Tuamotu, where the inhabitants die four times in succession. When a man dies, his spirit, his tupaupau, will search for his new home, a crevice deep down among the caves of the sea. And since he cannot immediately find it, he will return again to his former body. And this miracle the Tuamotuan captain had witnessed himself; he and upwards of a hundred others. When the body quivered and came to life again for the third time the dead man spoke. He told those about him not to bury him for another three days, unless his body should become mea pe, a bit ripe. But the French Governor of the Islands, who happened to be there, insisted on interment, notwithstanding the protests of the natives. Now two days later, when they returned to the grave, they saw the earth shake and quiver. Then they knew that the living man was scratching at the soil beneath. It was a thing most terrible, mea riaria.

The eyes of the Tuamotuan glistened. His back stiffened and he leaned forward as he crouched. His deep, vibrating voice trembled in the night. The engine throbbed. About the deck the natives slept, half-naked in their pareu, *their loin cloths. Others chattered and laughed, lying on the copra sacks stacked about the rudder-box in the cockpit.*

The half-caste supercargo leaned toward me and whispered: "Qu'ils sont kanaques, hein?"

April 24. About eighty miles away Tahiti nui, the main island, is plainly visible, lying pale and transparent above the ocean. The highest peaks are blanketed and the base melts into the milky sea.

Now Moorea, and now Maia, come into view. The lifeless heat beats down on the oily, glassy sea. The islands are curtained off by the clouds; fade and emerge again from white cumulus clouds, tumbling and swelling on the edge of the ocean.

Now it is night and Tahiti is still many miles away. The Tuamotuan captain and a petania, an adventist native missionary from the Island of Rurutu, are learnedly debating as to whether Jesus Christ ever came to America.

"How, then, could Christ have come to America, since it was not yet discovered? Nor for many years thereafter."

"But America existed before it was discovered; and Christ therefore could have found it, had he so wished."

"But why, then, was it never mentioned in the Gospels, by all his disciples and friends?"

"But it is mentioned in the Mormon Bible and that is the revealed evidence of its truth."

"Now because something is written in a book, there is no evidence of its truth. How can you know that these words were not lies, te mau parau haavare?"

"But the only evidence that you can show me that Christ did not come to America are the written words of your Bible. They, too, may lie."

I lay below on my pandamus mat, which I had spread over the copra sacks. Black popoti, enormous cockroaches, scurried over me. I meditated on certain aspects of contemporary art, which had been troubling me for a long time.

Such was the setting. Romance, poetry, myth and religion were woven into the colorful tapestry that was for two years the background of my first meditation on the meaning and purpose of Modern Art. That is as it should be. No thinking, of course, is pure, existing in a vacuum. It is conditioned by the impact on the human individual of his environment.

What first impelled me to give up law as a profession — before actually I had started to practice it — was the six months I spent cow-punching in Texas and riding with an Indian guide over the Sierras of Durango, Sinaloa, Sonora, and Chihuahua in Mexico. It was quite impossible for me in after years to explain to others the wealth of experience, the warmth of emotions, the bright colors which I had drawn from this short six months' adventure. What Melville's cruises in a deep-bottomed whaler among the palm-fringed atolls of the Pacific were to him, what that short summer's camping trip among the Indians of the Northwest was to Parkman, what it meant to Samuel Clemens to pilot a broad paddlewheeler through the snags of the Mississippi — all that to me were these months of panhandling, riding, roping and shooting north and south of the Rio Grande.

Fifteen years later, returning from the battlefields of France after World War I, I determined to isolate myself from contemporary art currents in order to catch up with lost time. Just as my short adventure in Texas and Mexico had been indirectly responsible for my quitting the law for art, so the two solitary years I spent in a remote Polynesian village gave me time to think at the moment in my life when I was groping for some sort of self-expression. That richness and fullness and oneness which are typical of all primitive societies impressed itself upon me. It was my lived experience from day to day which convinced me that art, most literally, is an expression of life. Never something isolated from it. Indeed, art is the most intense act of living. And it was from my own lived experience that my esthetics emerged and took shape. For the danger of purely mental speculation, divorced from experience, is barrenness. That wisest of men, Anatole France, once wrote: "Les vérités découvertes par l'intelligence demeurent stériles. Le coeur est seul capable de féconder son rêve . . . Si l'on raisonne, on ne s'envole jamais."

That spring in Tahiti I had been reading Clive Bell's provocative book on Modern Art. It both stimulated and troubled me. I was never quite happy or satisfied with his brilliant but superficial mind. I could not believe that a few pat phrases could thus disembowel art of what seemed to me its most vital content, life. The answer to the dead end which his logic raised suddenly burst upon me. That night, lying comfortably below on my copra sacks in the hold of the little schooner, I recorded in my diary:

"Art is not 'significant form.' It is nature translated into significant form, or design, as I prefer to call it. Painting and sculpture are the visible aspects of nature, translated into form. So each different expression of many-faceted nature will awaken a response through one or more of the senses, in that particular art medium best suited to interpret it. Music and the dance will interpret nature and life as they are apprehended by the ear or by that innate and universal sense of rhythm which pulses through all living things. The ear and mind, and the heart too, will translate nature into prose or poetry. We react to life in many ways; and may not each reaction have its own suitable expression in art?

"If it is true, let us suppose in a portrait by Rembrandt, that the entire esthetic significance lies in what Clive Bell calls 'significant form,' line, color and design; if the esthetic value of a painting is entirely divorced from its representational elements, why, then, would not this portrait be as esthetically satisfying, as beautiful, if these representational elements were entirely omitted? Do the insight into character, the human compassion, the tenderly poetic mood, the brooding philosophy, the face itself, add nothing to the esthetic content of the painting? According to Clive Bell and the apologists of the abstract painters and cubists, these qualities can logically be omitted from a picture, since they do not add to its esthetic content, its significant form. Why not omit the representation of nature from pictorial art?"

Artists are aware, more keenly than others, of the enduringly beautiful, the hidden sweetness, the intoxication of happiness, that life holds out to us; if we can but pluck the fruit from the bough. At moments, however, we feel that the world is about to enter — perhaps has already entered — a long, gray, and hopeless twilight; a nightmare of universal war, regression, ignorance, and barbarism. A sickly time for art and artists; for liberalism and the dignity of man. But from such a shadow of the dark ages, should it be upon us, only art — meager, shrunken and starved though it be — will survive. Art, more than ever, is important today; and artists should carefully consider where they are going; and their purpose and meaning in life.

I am old enough to have experienced or participated in five important art movements since the turn of the century. French Impressionism; the American Ashcan School; the School of Paris and Cubism during those early and exciting days when it first exploded on the world; Regionalism,

the Mexican Mural Movement, and the New Deal Subsidy of Art—
what we may loosely lump together as the social-conscious trend of the
twenties and early thirties; and lastly the postwar currents of contemporary art. I can recall with sentiment and pride my friendship with Mary
Cassatt when she was an old lady; my visits to Auguste Rodin and Aristide Maillol in their Paris studios, and to the latter in his home at Banyuls, where the Pyrenees taper off into the sea; the discussions about
French art and El Greco with John Sargent in his London house; and I
have often peered over the low stone wall at the aged Claude Monet, as
he sat painting on a canvas stool among his water-lilies and chrysanthe-
mums in his garden at Giverny-près-Vernon on the Seine. I have known
in greater or less measure many of the familiar figures of the Modern
European Movement: Jules Pascin, Fernand Léger, Marc Chagall, Chaim
Soutine, Albert Gleizes, George Grosz, Oskar Kokoschka, Emile Othon
Friesz, Constantin Brancusi, Ossip Zadkine, Max Ernst, and others. I
have listened to Gertrude Stein's brilliant, egocentric and pernicious
sophistry in the Rue de Fleurus, and to the tortuous, sincere and sopo-
rific monologues of her brother Leo at the Café du Dôme. With a few
exceptions I have known and talked to every important American and
Mexican artist of the past generation.

Such casual conversations and lasting friendships with a few of the
chief actors will not necessarily sharpen one's critical discrimination, but
they afford a body of evidence which may help one's understanding of
an important revolutionary movement.

All art is directly related to life; and the visual world is the subject
matter of the graphic and plastic artist, the painter and sculptor. In certain periods people have turned lovingly and with a curiosity to understand and identify themselves with nature and the visual world. Theirs
was the outgoing or extroverted approach. At other moments among
primitive people, in dark ages of despotism, of transition or of readjustment, man turned his eyes away from nature and looked inward for
some magic symbol or mystic faith that could propitiate or at least reveal
the meaning of a seemingly hostile world.

These two basic approaches to life seem always best to have expressed
themselves in two alternating and recurrent idioms of design, which we

can think of as the representational or extroverted and the abstract or introverted approach.

All great civilizations and all great art, however, show a healthy balance between the outward-looking preoccupation with the visual world and the inward spiritual need. Modern Art, which has created the most significant school of design since the Renaissance superseded the Gothic five hundred years ago, marks the end of a world cycle. Are its extreme manifestations a mere escape from an all-pervading world fear? Are they crystallizing into the language of another dark age? Or will the balance between Abstract Expressionism and the representational tradition achieve an art expression worthy of a happier and a better world?

Part I ᛯ Art Through the Ages

THE MANY-SIDED
MODERN MOVEMENT

From the Author's Diary, July 2, 1930. Sketching these last two months in Charleston, South Carolina. Negro nursemaids on the Battery, naked children in Catfish Alley, and the spring freshet of northern tourists at Timrod Inn. Late afternoons I played handball at Folly Beach with Peter Blume, who is making his preliminary sketches for "South of Scranton." I drove back alone through the Smoky Mountains and the hill towns of West Virginia. The dogwoods and Judas trees were no longer in blossom. The great evil-looking, white-ivory lips of the magnolia flowers had turned a rusty brown. The roads were thick with dust. The blue-shuttered Negro cabins leaned this way and that. On a Saturday afternoon the farmers and hired hands, seated on the steps of the county courthouses, stared at me and through me and then spat tobacco juice noncommittally between their mud-crusted boots. Everything was shabby and run-down, and hadn't changed too much since George Washington, riding north a century and a half before, had noted in one of his diaries the difference between southern one-crop cultivation and Pennsylvania-Dutch farm thrift.

That was the year that put-put golf swept like a prairie fire, soon to be extinguished, across the nation. Every little hillbilly town that could boast of a hotel and garage also advertised its put-put golf course. Another blight that year descended on these worm-eaten and somnolent little villages. Modern art, as a genuine American packaging device, had fluttered into the shoe stores, stationers, and pharmacies in a big way. All sorts of horrid useless little chromium knickknacks — cylinders, spirals and stepped-back platforms — were used as pedestals to display the shops' shoddy wares. As a friend of mine said, Modernism was retailed at any price; from the huge over-all effects filling the show windows and bought on the installment plan to the modest little sets with just room enough for a pair of slippers and a couple of neckties, selling at $1.98. It was somehow a pathetic guarantee that the modest wares on display were up-to-date. Americans, who are intellectually cautious, have a horror of being left too far behind the times. Modernism in its most unappetizing and pretentious form was accepted by Hollywood and small business all over the country a decade or so in advance of the angry discussions which recently sizzled among our artists over the jury selections of the Metropolitan Museum's exhibitions of contemporary art.

Peter Blume did not finish his "South of Scranton" until a year or so later. But I remember very well the dry, detailed pencil figure drawings that served as preliminary sketches and were pinned to the walls of his Charleston bedroom. Today the painting does not seem very radical or avant-gardist, completely representational as is its symbolism or fantasy, and charged with moral and political implications. But I remember the hubbub over it when it received the first prize at the Carnegie International (see Fig. 1). Often since then I have been puzzled comparing the excitement among art circles at the time with the placid acceptance of the extreme modernism in the shop windows of those sleepy little West Virginia and Smoky Mountain villages. Today there still remains the same paradox in Modern Art.

I believe that this curious reaction to Modernism — on the one hand its easy and unconscious acceptance in many phases of contemporary life by the most unsophisticated, and on the other the open hostility toward it and suspicion as to its validity among many educated and cultured persons — suggests a certain schizophrenia in our minds toward the movement, perhaps a certain ambivalence in the movement itself.

With a good deal of excitement and even more curiosity I had witnessed the first great Exhibition of Cubism in 1912. Although of course there have been many minor developments since then, it seems to me that by that date abstract art was a fully mature expression. The high hurdles had been taken and the most troublesome problems solved. Canvases from that period could be slid alongside many paintings today without seriously dating. In many cases they would pass as contemporary.

The common binder that united the different currents that went into the creation of Modern Art was of course the revolt against certain phases of the accepted art of the day. These phases, in the field of painting, we can loosely lump together as the current debased and outmoded schools of design — Victorian, neoclassic, or pseudo-baroque; the realistic approach to life of Impressionism and the prevalence of the sentimental-anecdotal in official art.

All this was an art tradition that no longer in any sense reflected the spirit of the times. For a generation artists had been showing a growing impatience and irritation with these outmoded styles. At the turn of the century this irritation exploded into a new style — Modern Design. But the new style was in a fluid and formative stage. In its expression we see evidence of the protest against and irritation with the past, as well as the clear indication of a new style.

Today we cannot surely say that the new world, the Modern Movement, is as yet sharply outlined and accepted in all its manifestations: in the fields of political thought, religion, education, and art. Some phases of modern life have become clearly recognized and are accepted. About other aspects of our civilization there are doubts and uncertainties. Modern Art also mirrors these uncertainties, frustrations and fears.

THE CREATIVE ACT
AND IMAGINATION

From the Author's Tahitian Diary, November 18, 1922. Charlie Nordhoff and James Norman Hall have lent me a copy of the nineteenth-century explorer J. A. Moerenhout's Voyages aux Iles du Grand Ocean, *first published in 1837. In it I came across the Tahitian text of an ancient Polynesian poem concerning the creation of the world, the immortality of the soul and the life hereafter. With the help of Paia, the minister, and Afereti, the schoolmaster, I have attempted to render it in English.*

Concerning Taaroa, the God Creator

Parahi; Taaroa te ioa.	He existed. Taaroa was his name.
Iroto i te aere;	He existed in the void;
Aita fenua; aita rai;	No earth; no sky;
Aita e tai; aita e taata.	No sea; no human being.
Pii Taaroa,	Taaroa calls aloud,
Areara aita roa.	But none answer.
Ona ae iho toreira e ua riro oia	
i te hoe noa.	He alone existed at that moment.
Te tumu Taaroa;	Taaroa was the basic origin;
Te papa;	The rocks;
Taaroa te one;	Taaroa the sands;
Oia o Taaroa iho tona ioa.	Taaroa was his very name.
Taaroa te ao;	Taaroa was the existing universe;
Taaroa te roto;	Taaroa, the central axis;
Taaroa te oteo;	Taaroa, the germ of life;
Taaroa te raro;	Taaroa, the very foundation;
Taaroa te tai;	Taaroa, the ocean beyond the land;
Taaroa te paari;	Taaroa, the ruggedly wise.
Fanau i te ao;	He it was that created the universe,
Te ao rahi e te moa,	The great and sacred universe,

Ei paa no Taaroa,
Te ori ori ra fenua.

As a shell for Taaroa,
To sing in harmony.

The Creation

E te tumu; e te papa;
E te one;
Matou teie.
Haere mai outou tei hamani i
  te fenua.
Pohia; popohia; aita e farerei.

Ye basic foundations, ye rocks;
Ye sands;
It is we.
Come hither, who shall create the
  land.
He urges them and urges them again
  but they will not unite.

Taaroa ona i te hitu rai ei hamani
  i te tumu matamua.

Then he hurls the seven firmaments
  in order to create the very foundation.

Fanau ai te rai;
Pau te poi;
Ua itea pauroa hia.
Te maramarama raa iropu i te ao.

The light of heaven was created;
Darkness was dispelled;
Everywhere there was light;
Lighted was the center of the uni-
  verse.

Ua maere te atua i te raa.

The god stood in admiration of the
  sight.

E pau te hauti raa;
E pau te afai parau;
E pau te orero raa.
E faa i te tumu;
E faa i te papa;
E faa i te one;
Ua ohu i te rai;
Ua tetei te rai;
Ia hohonu;
E pau te fenua i hamani hia.

His creative effort has ceased;
His words have been carried;
His words are spoken;
The basic origins are fixed;
The rocks are in place;
The sands are spread abroad;
The skies revolve;
The firmaments are suspended;
The sea lies in its depth;
The creation of the world is at an end.

For the imagination to create unity out of chaos! That is art: intuitive creation. And it is satisfying to think that human beings above or below the Equator, separated by great intervals of time or by the vast expanse of many oceans, should have had the same poetic dream about the first great act of creative splendor. Nevertheless the function of art in society has had a different meaning in every civilization and for each new generation. Since Plato wrote his *Symposium* there have been more than twenty different interpretations of art and beauty. Here are some of I. A.

Richards' definitions of what throughout the ages philosophers have found beautiful: Anything is beautiful which possesses the simple quality of Beauty; which has a specified Form (Clive Bell and the protagonists of the Modern Movement); which is a work of Genius (Kant and Schopenhauer); which reveals Truth, the Spirit of Nature, the Ideal, the Universal, the Typical (Plato); which produces Illusion; which leads to desirable Social effects (Ruskin); which is an Expression (Croce); which causes Pleasure (Herbert Spencer and Santayana); which promotes a Specific Emotion; or which heightens Vitality (Bergson).

Half a century ago Benedetto Croce published his *Estetica*. It had a great influence on contemporary European thought and expressed in simple terms the fundamental philosophy of Modern Art. There are only two forms of knowledge, said Croce; the intellectual and the esthetic. The intellectual form is the concept, the idea; and the highest form of intellectual knowledge is science, the affirmation of universal concepts. The esthetic form of knowledge is intuition or the imagination; and the summit of intuitive knowledge is art. There is much more to it, of course, than this; but it is important to remember that a few years before the Fauves painters of Paris burst into flame, Croce had spoken the keynote of their unwritten faith: the creative act is imagination; nothing else. Sir Herbert Read, the English critic, phrases the same idea: "The artist's exceptional faculties give him more than manual dexterity, more than sensuous refinement, that 'more' which is an intuition of the nature of reality and justifies us in regarding art as an indispensable mode of knowledge."

Jawaharlal Nehru, too, is aware of this other "intuition of the nature of reality"—Croce's intuitive approach to life through the imagination —when he writes: "It may be that the scientific method of observation is not always applicable to all the varieties of human experience . . . When both science and philosophy fail us, we shall have to rely on such other powers of apprehension as we may possess. For there appears to be a definite stopping place beyond which reason, as the mind is at present constituted, cannot go. 'La dernière démarche de la raison,' says Pascal, 'c'est de connaître qu'il y a une infinité de choses qui la surpassent. Elle est bien faible si elle ne va jusque-là.'"

1. Peter Blume. *South of Scranton.* Metropolitan Museum

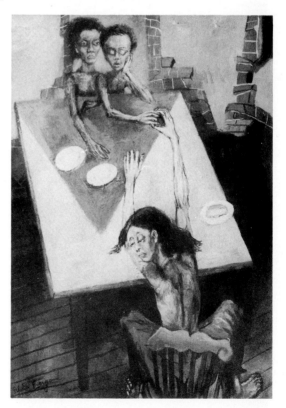

2. Philip Evergood. *Don't Cry, Little Mother.* A.C.A. Gallery

3. John Marin. *Taos, 1930.* McNay Art Institute

4. Charles Demuth. *Acrobats.* Museum of Modern Art

5. Paul Klee. *Saint of the Inner Light*. Museum of Modern Art

6. Ink drawing by a six-year-old child

7. Wax crayon drawing by an insane person

8. Pablo Picasso. *Three Musicians*. Museum of Modern Art

9. Max Weber. *Invocation*. Mr. and Mrs. Arthur Fleischman, Detroit

My friend, Phil Evergood, whose painting is always touched with lyric poetry, believes that great artists intuitively absorb the experience of life, before fusing it into an imaginative expression. "Odilon Redon touched a cobweb once, I can tell, and in his fingertips he retained that elusive memory of the sensation all his life . . . Rembrandt kissed the weather-beaten cheek of his old grandmother once, I can tell, and in his memory he retained the apple feel of the tight skin of her forehead and the downy wrinkled cheek with the rosy smear and the sharp tracery of etched lines around the eyes and the warm yellowish glow of the whole head."

To Croce, however, the work of art, the "artistic act" — a painting, poem or statue — is always something more than mere imaginative expression. It is imagination plus the practical act, let us say, of covering a canvas with paint or carving a shape from a block of stone. Pure expression, he argues, has merely intuition of things, but does not will them; and since intuition does not imply a desired end, it is incapable of employing means or techniques for that purpose. The artist sees a landscape; he has an intuitive response and then through an act of will he performs a practical act which results in a poem or a painting. Thus the work of art is no longer simply imaginative expression.

But can one thus dissect, carve apart, label, and pigeonhole the vague, subconscious elements of imagination, thought, and action which, fused together in the flow of a living operation, give birth to a child's drawing, or to the many-toned harmonies of a performance of one of Beethoven's symphonies? At what moment does the practical act begin and the intuitive, imaginative expression fade away, in the process that results in the final flowering?

I can answer this question only in terms of my own experience; and I believe it is that of other artists. Sitting before the easel with pen or brush in hand, I start drawing, timidly perhaps, or my thoughts elsewhere engaged, or again with a definite, rigid, and preconceived purpose. Then, of a sudden, if things go well, my pen begins to run, to flow, of itself, subconsciously, effortlessly; expressing something of me, through me, which I had not known to be there; which others will recognize as having the stamp of *my* drawing. What is it, if not automatic writing? This subconscious response was not merely an inner intuition. It flowed from my elbow, my wrist, the pressure of the shoulder. Yes, from the point, the weight of the pen itself. It is the muscular response of the pianist when he strikes a chord; of the tennis player when he hits the ball. An element of it was perhaps a predetermined act of will; another element was the instantaneously evoked visual reaction; and still a third was an automatic physical reflex. So, I believe, in the creation of one of Rembrandt's drawings, from the artist's imaginative response, from the muscular tension of his hand; perhaps from the contact of such inert physical substances as pen, ink, or paper, there flowed a spark of creative energy into something that was dead and started it pulsing with life for all time. Has not every artist — the poet, the musician, the sculptor — experienced this feeling with a shock of excitement: that his mind, his hand, his ear, was merely the channel through which some external compelling energy was operating, without his own intent or participation? To what extent did the drawing or the music write itself? To what extent did some external force flow into it?

I have often said that art is an intuitive reaction, or re-creation, or critique of life, expressed with a certain rhythm or design in different media; and that every aspect of life will have an art medium appropriate to its expression. This means again that every aspect or activity of life, when transformed through imagination, becomes a reflection or critique, the "outward visible sign" of the universe, expressive of the individual artist as well as the culture that produced it. The product of any activity, then, may be a work of art transcending the useful function of that particular object.

It is a commonplace to praise a cook by calling her a real artist; or by asserting that one's friend has made an art of living. But the real significance of the remark is less appreciated: that something other than pre-eminence in cooking or and understanding of the world has gone into the meal or into our friend's mode of living. The transcendent quality which raised Bill Tilden's tennis game to a work of art is exactly the same quality which lifts Titian's Pope Paul III (Fig. 10) from a commission portrait to a great creative masterpiece — imaginative expression. When a useful activity is sublimated into what John Dewey calls a personal experience; into Croce's "intuitive expression," into what I prefer calling an imaginative reaction to, or critique of, life — it has then another value. Since art reshapes and criticizes life through its selective reflection of the external world, it becomes a yardstick of man's mind, aspirations, religion, and philosophy. It is the only open-sesame by which we can penetrate the spiritual meaning of the great civilizations of the past and thus borrow from their wisdom and experience in recharting our course through the night that lies ahead.

Through French cooking we have a better awareness of the sobriety, the refinement, the esthetic approach of the French mind. The difference between cricket and baseball, between prize-fighting and the highly artistic ritual of Spanish bullfighting, between a Sicilian donkey-cart and an Indian snowshoe or an Adirondack canoe, is the difference between the environment, conditioning, minds, aptitudes, passions, and inclinations of nations. If it is true that art is the only light that casts a glimmer into the recesses of the past, it is also true that a civilization is reflected in its household crafts as well as — sometimes more spiritually than — in its Supreme Court buildings and battle monuments. Does one get closer to the wellsprings of American character, deficiencies, and genius through Walt Disney's Mickey Mouse and *The New Yorker* cartoons than through the neoclassic sterility of the Pennsylvania Triangle in Washington? That many-faceted thing called civilization is reflected in Walt Whitman's poetry, as it is also in the purity of the lines of clipper ships. The point to remember is that it is imagination which sublimates a useful thing, as well as a triumphal arch, into a work of transcendent and everlasting value.

For the moment it is wise then to remember, in the first place, that every form of art — the poem, painting, temple, novel, dance, or musical composition — was intended, when first created, to serve a useful purpose; and second, that the simplest craft object becomes a work of art when its creator has added to its useful purpose the transcendent quality of imagination. The difference, then, between art and craft is largely arbitrary, a difference in degree, inherent in social approach and in the immemorial and accepted use of language.

This distinction between "fine" and craft art did not exist in the Hellenic age. And certainly the distinction does not exist at all among primitive people. For to them the same love and concentration on technical perfection goes into the creation of an artifact or a statue or a ritualistic symbol charged with religious and supernatural significance.

In Tahiti I was struck by the fact that although the Tahitians' personal and social relations were often far more complicated and subtle than ours, and although they had a highly developed sensitivity in many fields of art, yet they had no understanding whatsoever of any abstract concept. As far as I know they had no distinguishing word at all for beauty. The closest they got to it was "a suitable thing" or "a proper thing" (*mea nehenehe*) — and nicely enough this was also their only phrase for any superlative expression such as "the best," "the loveliest," "the only," "the shortest," "the quickest," and so on. Naturally such forthright, objective, and yes-saying people would not bother their heads much over esthetics. Art to them was a ritualistic expression of some social activity. It might be said that it was all "craft" and all "fine."

Now in the age that lies ahead of us — in Asia as in Westchester County — this difference will perhaps be less apparent between museum and popular art; between grand opera and *Oklahoma!*; between murals for the United Nations and murals for the subways. The standards of art will not necessarily be lowered. I hope, however, that there will be a far greater audience participating in and enjoying the things of the spirit. They will not only create, but they will insist for their own entertainment on an art expression commensurable with their lives and understanding.

3 '

IMAGINATION AND METHOD

From the Author's Diary: May 2, 1939. I had spent the summer of 1915 and the following one at Giverny-près-Vernon in Normandy. Not so long out of art schools, I was floundering about, beginning to appreciate the gulf that separates the student from the mature artist. In the narrower sense my student period lay behind me. I could by now adequately construct exhibitable paintings, belonging to a definite tradition, yet with some slight personal approach in design, color, or treatment. I was still, of course, essentially interested in technique. I was then and for several years thereafter under the spell of Mary Cassatt, and of Degas, whom she, too, so greatly admired. At night with a bottle of white Pouilly at my elbow I would study photographs of their work and would consciously pose my models the next day as they had posed theirs.

Once or twice during the summer my friend Frederick Carl Frieseke would criticize my work. On one such visit to my studio in August 1916, he paused for several moments in front of a canvas I had just finished of a seated nude with black stockings. I became a little nervous and to cover my apprehension asked with a smile: "Do you find it almost as good as a Degas?"

This upset Fred very much. I could see that he was angry. He looked at me a little indignantly. He was the most sensitive and sincere man that ever lived, and he resented imitation as much as he cherished his own probity in art. He waited a moment and then said: "No. It does not. It looks—almost —like a Biddle."

He had taught me a lesson. Before this I had never so clearly apprehended the distinction between method or craft and imagination. And yet I had been very much aware of the difference in approach of even the most gifted student and that of a creative artist. At Julian's Academy, which still retained its high standard of academic draftsmanship, the highest praise would be: "He draws —or paints—almost as well as X." And one only strove to emulate "les anciens." Yet the day a student left the school and was on his own, the most devastating criticism of his work would be: "Yes, clever; but a little reminiscent of Y., don't you think?" For the ambitious student strives only to imitate and equal another. The artist with probity wants only to be himself.

I have said that art is the intuitive or imaginative recreation of life. But what is imagination? Nothing other than that most rare and heaven-born gift of seeing life with fresh eyes. It is to hear new rhythms, accords, meanings; to sense new directions in time-worn words, and sounds and human situations. It is to respond freshly, differently, creatively to our old, old world.

There is nothing, then, magical or supernatural about imagination or even genius, other than its extreme and therefore tragic infrequency. We must always remember that its significance is one of degree and quality. It goes against my instincts to conceive of a normal child without some spark of imagination; and even in older persons through the prism of love the drabbest gray can glisten like a rainbow. But one can never raise oneself from the floor by one's bootstraps. The child, gifted with intuitive self-expression, can re-create life only in childish images. The God of the Old Testament was no whit nobler, his beard no silkier, than the vision of the Hebrew prophets and poets who fashioned him. The Mexican mural movement, for many reasons the most important art expression of our century, is philosophically no more profound than the outlook on life of the genial, passionate, and childlike minds that were part of it.

Winston Churchill once told his son, politically minded but unaware of the need for arduous preparation of campaign oratory, that something other than whisky went into his own speeches. And it is true that more goes into a masterpiece than genius or imagination. The process of creation is as varied as are the personal habits of human beings. But by and large they follow the same pattern. There is a response to some disclosure of nature, some incident in life. Something presses the button. The artist in a flash may see the thing he wants to create; perhaps vaguely, the pattern emerging here and there from an impenetrable nothing; perhaps with the lucid clarity of a nightmare. Usually at the start the work will flow easily and subconsciously. But a moment inevitably comes in the doing, when the thing in his hands is dying. The poem that started writing itself cannot find the word to end the line. The painting that flowed over the canvas will not move. The artist's vision has blacked out. The composer no longer hears his melody rise from the little silent skeletons lying on the ruled lines. It is then that to breathe life into a deflated and inanimate thing, the artist must marshal every quality at his command, mental or moral, *other than imagination*: the experience of his life's work, of other successful ventures, skill in the techniques, the knowledge of past and present, fortitude, faith, and persistency. From these sources he must draw, as well as from that spring "higher than his tap."

It was old General Israel Putnam who admonished his men, "Trust in God and keep your powder dry." And powder, it seems to me, suggests very well that explosive force which we insist on in a work of art; that "something more," which there must be to move us. Yet all the powder in the world will hardly shoot a pea across the road. It is the rifled barrel that adds distance and gives direction to one's aim. There is no way, alas, of adding to the allotted charge of dynamite. All we can do is to guard it well from moisture. We need not squander the little that is served out as our portion. We can, however, improve the rifling of the barrel. And this is, in the broadest sense, our technical, intellectual, and moral equipment. We can polish and file; we can sharpen, whittle, and pare; we can clean our palette — we can shift our approach and raise our aim. And then we can only pray that there is still a little powder left when we pull the trigger.

But even if the powder is dissipated and the source of inspiration dry, the trained artist is still capable of an honorable performance. He can turn out a good "academy." This word, which is used almost universally in an insulting and derogatory sense, has its more respectable connotation — one which I cannot find in the dictionary, but which is known to every art student in life class. The worthy sense of "academy" is honest, skilled and traditionally accepted craft, though uninventive and without inspiration. It is comforting also to know that "craft" is derived from a word which originally meant strength and also cunning. Good line, color and design; good painting, sculpture, writing and music, without imagination — and how infinitesimal a fraction has it — is nothing other than academic craft. It forms the larger portion of every artist's work. For painting becomes academic the moment an artist repeats himself. Craft is, however, the basis, foundation and rock upon which the creative artist must stand before he takes off in a flash of creative imagination. We should never be ashamed of good craft or good academy. It is only when something vulgar or sickly has insinuated itself into the performance that it may become a little rotten. And also — in modern as in traditional art — when it has become dishonest craft.

Perhaps I can best illustrate the quality of imagination, which clothes with new images, ideas, shapes, and sounds the shopworn aspect of this stale world, by instances that have come to me from fellow artists. George Grosz told me a charming anecdote of an accomplished and greatly honored German landscapist who invariably started his landscapes by establishing the right color tone for the sky. But before mixing his colors he always prayed for a moment. If the color for the sky was right, the rest of the thing was easy sailing. I like the story. The old man seemed to know that all the skill in the world could not by itself establish the right tone of blue, even for a blue, blue sky, unless he could evoke that "something more" to go into it.

Charles Demuth, always a little satiated with life, wanting always so much more out of it than painting, yearning perhaps for the sort of debauchery through which he could float with absolute refinement, indulging indeed in his most intemperate excesses with a sense of perfection and artistry, used to say of himself and of John Marin with deprecating gaiety but rare penetration: "Marin and I drew our inspiration from the same source, French modernism. He took his up in bucketfuls, but he spilt most of it along the way. I could only carry mine in a teaspoon, but I never spilt a drop."

There you have it. Gunpowder and the rifling. Creative imagination and craft. And to make the proper choice of one's fowling piece one should, as I think is the case with Marin and Demuth, give careful consideration to the quality of one's explosive content (see Figs. 3 and 4 for examples of their work).

In the winter of 1925 Marsden Hartley, another early exhibitor with Demuth and Marin at Alfred Stieglitz' "291" Gallery, shared my studio at 84 Rue d'Assas in Paris. This unhappy, tormented, violent, proud, and bitter man united many of the traits of his two friends. Like Demuth he was hypersensitive, sensuous, and sophisticated in his tastes. He, too, had explored the shadowy depths of life and tasted the forbidden fruits of the night. But while such pleasures had dulled but not warped Demuth's sunny charm and appetite for life, they seemed to have embittered and corroded Marsden's deeply New England being. At any rate, although in his critical perception of the work of others he showed the most precious, refined, and *fin de siècle* taste, yet in his own work he seemed to thrash about in a torment of explosive, unchanneled, and inarticulate agony. That winter he had just returned from the south of France and was working from memory sketches on a series of huge, forbidding, and shapeless mountain scenes that seemed far better to illustrate Dante's *Inferno* than the sunlight of the Alpes Maritimes. He would come late to the studio, paint furiously for a few hours without saying a word; often finishing a large canvas at a sitting.

I used to think of Marsden sometimes, as did others of his friends, as essentially a poet, unable to express himself in the medium of paint. Before he died a few years ago Hartley had explored almost every avenue of modernism. It is pleasant to think that at the end, returning to his native state and a simpler and more robust idiom of expression, he was able to sum up with force and distinction the ways over which he had traveled and his deeply ingrained New England respect for life's integrity.

I have often wondered why it is that during the past century so many great artists have had to stumble through life with an equipment so inadequate for the weight of their message. Cézanne and Van Gogh were pathetically aware of their limitations, and painfully struggled for a mastery of technique, copying old masters, visiting museums, insisting again and again on the need of a faithful study of nature. The world has too often stamped with the imprimatur of genius or originality what was nothing more than the awkward and tortured expression of the artist's search for truth. I once asked Aristide Maillol's wife why the artist had pinned to his wall reproductions from some fashion magazine. "It is to help him correct his drawing," the good woman replied. "In Banyuls it is difficult to find models who will pose in the nude."

Five years ago I did a portrait of Yasuo Kuniyoshi in his studio at 30 East Fourteenth Street. Invariably when I start a portrait my nerves are strung to the breaking point, comparable, I suppose, to the tension of a prize-fighter about to enter the ring. Unhappily my blood pressure does not immediately subside after shaking hands with my adversary. Yas had an extremely interesting face, sensitive yet veiled, intransigent, sly, moody, and impenetrable. But he was something of a prima donna and his occasional irritability did not make him an easy sitter. As I began to work my nervous tension was almost physical pain. My mind seemed paralyzed. But when at last the thing got going, I could relax. We then exchanged ideas about many phases of American art, our opinions of contemporary painters and their approach to technical problems. Kuni-yoshi worked long hours but turned out very little; he having had a high standard of perfection. I asked him how he could paint so slowly. He said: "I sit most of the time looking at my canvas, waiting until I know what to do next. If something goes wrong, I always scrape down and wash out with turpentine." This happens essentially to be my own ap-proach. It is not necessarily the best one. There are many ways of pre-paring the earth in the hopes that a seed will germinate in it.

Alec Brook and I painted each other in the winter of 1929. He had covered his large canvas with a soup of paint in a couple of hours. He was on his feet the whole time, pacing back and forth in what seemed much too small a cage for him. Each noon he scraped out everything he had done during the previous hours. The whole thing ended, to me quite miraculously like a conjurer's trick, in the last half-hour's assembly of the many false or tentative starts of the previous sittings. Many artists — John Sargent, José Clemente Orozco — have worked in this way. It is as if the seat of their imagination and other mental faculties were in their hands and feet rather than in their brain cells. Maurice Sterne has told me that he never knew what one of his easel pictures would be until it was "pulled together" at the finish.

I recall a conversation I had with Saint-John Perse —Alexis Léger — one August day in 1950 when he came to my studio at Truro on Cape Cod. Léger, like all great artists, is dogmatic, frequently prejudiced, but illuminating in his criticism; since what he says is not merely an objective analysis of another artist's work, but always takes on the color of his own creative approach.

I showed him a few of my recent paintings, telling him the great difficulty I had in satisfying myself. How I would sometimes eat out the entire background with paint and varnish remover and paint it in again. And this four or five times before I am happy. He said: "That is because you are maturing. You are more *exigeant*." But he also felt that I was too preoccupied with tonal relations and was sacrificing the "elliptical," imaginative, creative, subconscious approach to technical perfection. I answered it was true that recently I had become obsessed with tonal relations and a brighter, clearer palette. "But," I said, "when an artist strikes a lucky vein, he should keep at it for all it is worth — exhaust the last bit of ore. Then he can make a new approach. His development comes from the swing in one direction and then another."

"It is just that personal and particular participation," answered Léger, "that destroys the work of art. The artist should think only of the growth of the painting, the poem; never of his own attitude toward it."

I answered that of course the essence that gives the painting its ultimate importance is the subconscious, imaginative approach. But this the artist cannot will. He can only make sure that he is honest, true to himself, and tend his craft.

Both of us were right. I quote Léger because what he said reflects the attitude of a great artist toward imagination. I have always recognized that a work of art once created has a life of its own. Has it a life of its own in the process of creation? I believe so.

During a recent year's stay in Rome I had the rare privilege of renewing an earlier and casual acquaintance with George Santayana. In his somewhat shabby and overcrowded bedroom in the Convent of the Blue Nuns I listened with respectful and fascinated excitement to the brilliant, enigmatic and solitary philosopher. He reminisced about his student days at Harvard in the eighties and his relations with President Eliot, Barrett Wendell, Henry and William James and others. But what interested me even more were the intimate revelations about his own works and human relations. Two themes seemed woven in recurring pattern in his talk. Although he was in his eighty-ninth year, almost blind and deaf, and actually dying of stomach cancer, he radiated charm, kindly tolerance, humor and a friendly acceptance of life. Yet more than once he spoke of his loneliness in life, the few friends he had made in America, his early pessimism, and later his complete withdrawal from the world.

The other theme, to which he constantly alluded, as if it had been an emotional disturbance in his early years, was the conflict between poetry and philosophy in his own creative expression. Of *The Sense of Beauty,* that masterful work on esthetics which first gave him a reputation, he said with a note of gay deprecation: "But it never would have been published if Barrett Wendell, who was on my side of the barricades against the solid phalanx of learning, had not sold it to Scribner's. There was not much philosophy in it, you know. At that time I was interested in poetry." He could never forgive President Eliot for having kept him waiting nine years before he made him an associate professor, and another nine years before he made him a full professor. "He always felt I had not enough solid learning. And I guess perhaps he was right. Poetry in those days was my real expression."

The last occasion on which I saw him, four months before his death, he told me that he had been reading Ovid that morning. The talk had drifted to William and Henry James. Santayana said: "I remember once, as William James was lecturing, his stepping to the open window and sniffing the spring air; and then saying that he would like to get some of that quality into his talk. But the story became apocryphal and was attributed to me. I was always accused of getting too much poetry into my lectures. You know Mr. Eliot hated me; but Palmer and Wendell were on my side. It was Palmer who told me I should model my poetry on Latin rather than Greek verse."

George Santayana wrote some charming early verses. He was a great philosopher. Irwin Edman has suggested that part of his greatness was the poetic beauty and imagination which he breathed into the driest of metaphysical abstractions. He got the "quality of the spring air into his lectures."

One could add many more examples to suggest, thus elliptically, the meaning of imagination. I have selected these few to give, if possible, a clearer understanding of this elusive form of knowledge; and the ways in which it may color and transform humble acts and also great creations.

TO MIRROR LIFE;
TO FORECAST HISTORY

From the Author's Diary: January 24, 1948. X asked me if I had seen the Picasso exhibition across the street. I said to him: "I should like to ask you two questions. Do you believe that there are ten thousand art students and commercial designers in the country who could turn out as good a performance in a fortnight?" He turned and twisted with all his Parisian charm. "Ah, Biddle après tout; il y a des qualités; une richesse d'invention; fécondité plastique; etc., etc." I smiled. "And secondly; do you think that the artist who painted those canvases is sincere?" — "Ah ça! J'ai connu Picasso depuis quarante ans, etc." I said: "Y., who has also known him for many years, thinks differently. He has told me that Picasso is foncièrement un cabotin." "Y.," he cried, "is corrupt. He is interested in nothing but money. He has sold many Picassos at a huge profit. He is deeply involved in the eighteenth century and ça ne cloche pas avec le modernisme." I said: "Have you read Leo Stein's Appreciation? He also from the very beginning gave Picasso 'des qualités!' Stein was among the first to buy his paintings. He insists that Picasso had great talent. He merely denies that he had character, integrity, or unusual intelligence." I added: "C'est une âme torturée et diabolique. Il veut tout déchirer; tout anéantir." "Ah ça," he answered, "vous avez raison."

In the winter of 1936, while teaching at the Colorado Springs Fine Arts Center, I was asked to review two groups of prints that were being simultaneously exhibited there. One was an exhibition organized by the Artists' Congress, under the title "America Today." The other was a distinguished and carefully selected group of black-and-white works by the foremost contemporary European artists. I was much struck at the time by the basic difference in approach between the American art of that period and the best work of the Ecole de Paris. Of the one hundred American prints, seventy-four dealt with the American scene or with some social criticism of American life; six with strikes or with strike-breakers; six with dust, sand, erosion, drought and floods. There were no nudes, no portraits and two still lifes. In contrast with the socially critical attitude of the American group, there was not one example among the distinguished Paris contemporaries — Matisse, Picasso, Dérain, Fernand Léger, Braque and the others — that seemed to me preoccupied with life at all; let alone social problems. The Paris artists were interested only in art; art for art's sake. I did not in my review of the two shows draw any inferences. What interested me was to chart the main currents in contemporary American art of that decade. During the depression and the early New Deal days, regionalism and social awareness had an enormous and not unhealthy influence on American art. But it would be very wrong if one were to infer from this that French Modernism, even escapist art and the Ivory Tower, does not reflect life.

At first glance, I suppose, there has been no art expression in European history which seems as little concerned with life as certain phases of Modern Art. It is very curious, then, in reading the early manifestoes of the Cubists and Futurists, to note how insistent they were on the role of their new stylistic language as a more suitable vehicle for the interpretation of life. One could almost say they seemed to consider this as the principal justification of the new idiom. That their linear abstractions were a source of esthetic pleasure hardly seems to have occurred to them. Why were they under the compulsion to assert so noisily that nature is apperceived in terms of the sphere, the cube and the cylinder? The Futurists, too, proclaimed that since we see objects, in motion, from different angles and successively in time, visual reality is more truthfully transcribed by an abstraction of nearly parallel elliptical lines and planes radiating from a constantly moving center; and not, as we had supposed, as seen through the eye of the camera. But were such questionable assertions a necessary credo for a new school of graphic design?

I had always thought of Paul Klee as a sensitive and inventive *petit maître,* with the most unerring, distinguished, and sensuous feeling for texture, medium, material, color, and design. Notwithstanding the profound and legitimate influence he had exercised on his generation, I considered him, and still do, as something light, gay, witty and refined. Yet Klee was both mystic and philosopher. He felt that in his art he was interpreting — literally or through symbols — the hideous crises through

which his world was passing; despair, hope, evil, and the hidden meaning of the universe (see Fig. 5). Carola Giedion-Welcker, who knew
him personally, writes that even as a young artist he "had grasped the
central problem of the epoch: the priority in painting of the spiritual content." Kandinsky, too, the most abstract of the abstract, in his book *Ueber
das Geistige in der Kunst,* as early as 1912 writes of the "basically mystic
in construction." And many young American nonobjective artists of the
present decade are obsessed with the conviction that they are expressing
the ultimate realities of life, and even religious revelations, in their painting.*

It is very important to remember that the creators of what often seems
the most detached and abstract art have sought for new idioms of expression, not primarily because they were concerned with their esthetic
beauty, but because they considered them a clearer vehicle with which
to interpret life. And this same critical justification occurs in other art
media. When Amy Lowell wrote her work on the French Symbolist
poets, her plea for a more sympathetic understanding of them was that
the new images took the place of clichés that had become meaningless;
and gave a cleaner, clearer, more honest interpretation of life. And surely
the burden of criticism in the many books and articles on James Joyce's
Ulysses or the prose of Gertrude Stein has always been: "But that is actually what happens inside one's mind"; rather than "But what lovely
ringing prose, even if it doesn't seem to make sense." And similarly the
architects, who with the painters, the musicians and the poets, were
struggling with a new stylistic idiom, defended it for almost a generation

---

* "When I create a painting, drawing, etc., I attempt to assemble what seems to me
significant form through the use of lines, colors, shapes, and design. These elements
become significant to me when I find a certain relationship between them and the philosophic, sociological, and esthetic patterns with which I am concerned. In painting, I
create, then, shapes and colors which, emotionally, I can relate to these patterns. Naturally I do not suppose or intend that my paintings should have the same meaning or
'message' for the spectator. But I do intend that my paintings, though abstract, should
reveal their concern with the predicament in which man finds himself . . ." (Robert
Neuman, in *Contemporary American Painting,* 1952, Urbana: University of Illinois
Press, 1952).
   "[Stuart Davis'] purpose is to create forms that embody the psychological content
of his perceptions and emotions in response to that subject matter. . . They are organized in a way that expresses the psychological temper of some aspect of the society
he lives in and of his own temperament in relation to that society" (Ralph Pearson,
The Modern Renaissance in American Art, New York: Harpers, 1954).

with the somewhat superfluous excuse that its approach was merely functional; not that it was expressive design.

I wish to make two points, both of which are often forgotten. Many artists — at a guess I should say most — believe that their work carries some ulterior, transcendent message not spelled out in literal terms in their pictures, their music or their stories. And this of course is as true of the nonobjective artist as of Renoir, Degas, Rubens or Giorgione. But it is also true, whether the artist recognizes it or not, that an approach to life itself, a personal reflection of it, is indicated in his paintings. The Venetian, Dutch and Flemish painters of the sixteenth and seventeenth centuries reflected life by loving it. The French Impressionists reflected life by looking at it — with fresh eyes. Perhaps our own artists are thinking about life. Their thoughts are a little muddled and chaotic, but those thoughts are a reflection of this our world.

Picasso, who has flashes of insight, when not engaged in clowning, said: "The artist is a receptacle for emotions, regardless of whether they spring from heaven, from earth, from a scrap of paper, from a passing face, or from a spider's web."

George Grosz writes in his autobiography, *A Little Yes and a Big No*: "I felt tradition had died and that art was in a state of flux . . . The seeds of decay existed in every one of us. The best and greatest artists participated joyously in the general destruction . . . Spengler exerted quite an influence on me and made me aware of the fact that instead of being in a temple of art I was at the clearance of a huge warehouse . . . My own hopes never lay with the masses . . . I lived high up in an attic studio, closer to the stars, the moon and the birds than to people.

"I drew drunkards; puking men; men who had murdered women, sitting on their coffins playing skat, while within the coffins could be seen their bloody victims. I drew a man, face filled with fright, washing blood from his hands . . . I drew lonely little men fleeing madly through empty streets . . . I drew soldiers without noses; war cripples with crustaceanlike steel arms . . . a colonel with his fly open, embracing a nurse; a medical officer emptying into a pit a pail filled with various parts of the human body . . ."

I have known George Grosz for over twenty-five years. Hidden under

the savagery, the cynicism and the "Big No" of his defense is a tenderness and romantic innocence that was never quite blunted by the youthful impressions of World War I and the despair that settled over Germany in the years that followed (see Fig. 15). And I have suspected, too,
that Ernest Hemingway's adolescent tough-guy attitude and often immature boy-scout preoccupation with death cover up some early childhood
memory, when he first saw a cat play with a mouse and ran screaming to
his nurse in the hope that she could blot out such horror.

If the splintering, radiating, centrifugal design of Cubism had been
born of the postwar years, if the "dehumanization" of Modern Art had
been originally a reflection and expression of war-torn Europe, we could
more easily understand it. The extraordinary thing about the movement
— which we similarly note in the fields of music, architecture, and poetry
— was that it germinated in the first years of the century and was a fully
matured expression before World War I. Only such artists as have grown
up in those secure and placid years will remember how untroubled was
their thinking by moral problems or a compulsive sense of guilt. Indeed
Henry Varnum Poor has insisted — and with every justification — that as
great a force as Modern Art could only have developed in a period when
artists were free from anxiety and could create in peace.

It has always been clear that great artists can alter the pattern of history. The pen is mightier than the sword. Beaumarchais, Voltaire and
Rousseau were as responsible for the outbreak of the French Revolution
as were the tax on salt and the suffering of the peasants. It seems to me
quite plausible, then, that a great art movement, manifesting itself along
similar emotional patterns in various fields of expression, should reflect
the world's hidden spiritual sickness; even though the disease had as yet
not broken out; reflect the slow agony of a long and dying period of history and foreshadow the birth pains of a new cycle. And this I believe to
be the case.

In one of Emile Zola's novels, *L'Oeuvre*, the hero of which was modeled on Paul Cézanne, the painter and a friend at one point discuss the
attitude of the revolutionary, avant-gardist artist toward the traditional
movement from which he has made his escape. "But, alas," cries his

friend, "no matter how successfully you believe that you have thrown off
the shackles of the past, you can never completely do so. The fact that
you have an antagonist binds you to his ideas, which you wish to destroy.
Only the next generation, freed from the obsessions of the past, can look
untroubled into the future and create its dreams."

To understand the Modern Movement we must always bear in mind
this dual direction of its creative energy. Modernism has destroyed—
ended for all time—idioms, standards, and ideals that the world clung to
for five centuries. To accomplish this it has dissipated much creative energy. It is only when such energy is set free for purely imaginative expression and is not channeled into negative protests, that the real character of this movement will be clearly outlined.

When the shrewd old peasant-sculptor Constantin Brancusi, caress-
ing with his gnarled workman's hand the subtly chiseled perfection of
his bronze abstractions, shouted to his *haut monde* Parisian admirers that
Michelangelo is nothing but raw meat—"C'est du biftek"; when Frank
Lloyd Wright sneers at a New York gathering of distinguished architects:
"I see that you fellows are still playing around with cornices"; when Picasso thumbnoses a bewildered audience of idolators by his clowning and
"diabolism"; when George Grosz tries to hide his German sentiment and
romantic warmth by "puking" on the world—are not these sensitive and
talented artists protecting themselves against the obsession of an outworn
order they wish to destroy? Do they perhaps express the chaos of a time
without clearly crystallized beliefs and an accepted stylistic idiom? Is
there also a negative side to Modern Art?

This dual, two-faced aspect of modernism has never been given sufficient consideration. Artists themselves are often unaware of it. I can best
illustrate what I have called its negative and positive expression by briefly
outlining two brilliant and provocative books, José Ortega y Gasset's *Dehumanization of Art,* published in 1925, and Sigfried Giedion's *Space,
Time and Architecture,* published in 1941. Ortega observes that nineteenth-century art was largely romantic and realistic and therefore essentially human; and that the new movement in its attempt to "purify art"
from such extraneous elements was forced to a "progressive elimination
of the human." We then have an "art for artists and not for the masses,

for quality and not for hoi polloi." In his analysis of art itself, Ortega reasons that the observer must concentrate either on the object or on the work of art; but he can never do so on both simultaneously. Consequently the "preoccupation with the human content of the work is incompatible with esthetic enjoyment proper . . . Perception of 'lived' reality and perception of artistic form . . . are essentially incompatible."

The new art, Modern Art, became a purification, "a progressive elimination of the human, all too human, elements predominant in romantic and naturalistic productions. And in this process a point can be reached in which the human content has grown so thin it is negligible. We then have an art which can be comprehended only by the people possessed of the peculiar gift of artistic sensibility." Such is the case today. Modern Art is appreciated by a small minority of initiates. It is heartily disliked by the masses.

In the fields of music and literature we can observe the same elimination of the human element. "Beethoven and Wagner were realistic, and so was Chateaubriand as well as Zola. Seen from the vantage-point of our day Romanticism and naturalism draw close together and reveal their common realistic root . . . In Wagner, melodrama comes to a peak . . . Music had to be released of private sentiments and purified in an exemplary objectification. This was the deed of Debussy . . . So decisive is this conversion of the subjective attitude into the objective that any subsequent differentiations appear comparatively negligible. Debussy dehumanized music, that is why he marks a new era in the art of music."

We note the same trend, argues Ortega, in the field of literature. "Poetry had to be disencumbered of its human matter, which was dragging along, skirting the ground and bumping into trees and housetops like a deflated balloon. Here Mallarmé was the liberator . . . He 'eschewed' — as he said himself — the 'materials offered by nature.'"

What specifically are the distinguishing features of dehumanization, which Ortega finds in Modern Art?

The modern painter is not just clumsy in his portrayal of nature, as is the primitive or the early Christian fresco painter of the catacombs. Nor does he simply avoid nature as did the Moslem artists under the prohibition of the Koran. "He is brazenly set on deforming reality, shattering its human aspect . . . The art of which we speak is inhuman not only because it contains no things human, but also because it is an explicit act of dehumanization . . . The question is not to paint something altogether different from a man, a house, a mountain, but to paint a man who resembles a man as little as possible . . ."

Briefly, this is the pattern which the author of *The Revolt of the Masses* saw in the Modern Movement. Ortega's dilemma and the pessimism of his thesis lie in the fallacy of his major premise: that one cannot at the same time be interested in both human reality and the esthetic form. And this substantially is the fallacy of Clive Bell's esthetics and the fallacy which today pervades and vitiates so much of the criticism in all the fields of Modern Art. Pared down to its core it is the belief that art can be — must be — divorced from life and human experience.

I have already stated my own conviction that art is the integration of life with an abstract rhythm — form — and that esthetic enjoyment comes from a realization of this integration. Perception of lived realities and form are not, then, incompatible, and the "purification of human, all too human, elements, predominant in romantic and naturalistic productions," was not essential to Modern Art. The essential for a Modern Art was the purification of the bathos, false sentiment and triviality of the current academic realism, which was so completely without form. What was even more essential was the creation of a new style in design, a new interpretation of the organic meaning of the age, and fresh eyes capable of a yes-saying vision.

It is undoubtedly true that the "purification of the human," along with the creation of a new style, is characteristic of much Modern Art. This dehumanization was not germane, however, to the positive contribution of the movement. It is rather its negative destructive aspect — the protest against the "shackles of the past" which still obsesses us, and the feeling of insecurity in a troubled world which breeds a fear of life itself. For many of the best modern artists are today as concerned with the drama of life as ever were Hogarth or Daumier. I have in mind Ben Shahn, Max Weber, and much of Kuniyoshi's late work; also Phil Evergood, Abe Rattner, George Grosz, Jacob Epstein, William Zorach, Henry Poor and others. No great creative act or creative movement was ever negative, and Modernism is a great creative expression. Do not let us fool ourselves into thinking that dehumanization is a necessary part of it. Indeed Ortega concludes: "Who knows what may come out of this budding style? . . . Whatever their shortcomings, the young artists have to be granted one point: there is no turning back. The objectives would have to be supplemented by something positive: a suggestion of another way for art different from dehumanization and yet not coincident with the beaten and outworn paths."

In these same distinguishing characteristics of Modernism, in which Ortega has traced a pattern of dehumanization, Sigfried Giedion finds a prophetic imaginative content, which is the true expression of our times. Sigfried Giedion is an architect, a friend of Le Corbusier; and has written extensively on the relation of Modern Architecture to painting, mathematics and other fields. He believes that "in some periods there has existed a unity of culture. In those periods imagination and the external world flowed into one another." Society was essentially whole, balanced and mature. So was the art that gave expression to its culture. But in the past century this "unity subsisting between methods of thought and feeling" was destroyed by the philosophy of *laisser faire* materialism, in which there was little place for man's emotional and imaginative life. In the nineteenth century unrestricted production, and in the twentieth unrestricted power, became an end in itself. Thus, Giedion points out, the paths of science and the arts diverged; the connections between the methods of thinking and methods of feeling were broken. "The engineer remained subordinate to and detached from the architect. The architect, on the other hand, was left isolated from the most important movements going on in the world about him."

Giedion reasons that Modern Architecture with a new time element, fourthdimensional space, is the successful attempt to give imaginative expression to the organic needs of our times. In any given civilization the same imaginative approach to life manifests itself in different arts and fields of thought. We find this same space-time concept in Einstein's mathematical formulae, in James Joyce's *Ulysses,* and in Cubist painting. For painting, Giedion believes, is perhaps the most sensitive of all the arts; and the early work of the Cubists and Futurists, of Mondrian, Picasso, Braque, Arp, and others, would seem to anticipate the directions which architecture was to follow a decade later.

His clear, reasoned and documented analysis of the Modern Movement suggests that it is a sincere, imaginative expression of our age; and that it will help to integrate the emotional and intellectual outlets of the human being. What Giedion fails to see — as Ortega y Gasset failed to see — is that Modern Art is not all of it a single impulse expressing the organic needs of our times. That of course is its positive, constructive utterance. It also reflects the negative aspects of the age — the blows leveled at the ghosts of yesterday, the frustrations of the hour and the uncertainties of tomorrow.*

* "An unstable society such as ours cannot produce a Golden Age — all that we can hope is that this period be one of transition towards something better than we now have" (*The Northwest Architecture of Pietro Belluschi*).

5

FIXED STARS AND
REVOLVING COMETS

From the Author's Diary: April 11, 1952. We visited the Palazzo Municipale of San Sepolcro, which houses Piero della Francesca's "Resurrection of Christ" (Fig. 11). The Palazzo had been heavily bombed during the war and the plaster to either side of the fresco had crumbled away. Masons were chipping away the wall in the work of reconstruction. There seemed some evidence that the panel was not solidly anchored into the original wall, but had been subsequently installed there.

I was moved, standing before this small, isolated, fragmentary masterpiece, as nothing perhaps in Italy has moved me. The fresco, as with many great Renaissance murals, has no particular architectural relation to its setting. The composition of the painting is static, based on the traditional motif of the pyramid. The drawing is realistic, especially in the faces, and quite wooden in the figures and details of the landscape. The design is entirely without that animated and crowded orchestration of the "Legend of the Cross," which we saw two days ago in the Church of San Francesco at Arezzo. In the hands of anyone else I felt that the work would have been quelconque — *quite ordinary. But here the tension, nobility, simplicity and that inevitable "something more" raises it to a very great masterpiece. A hair's breadth between the mediocre and the truly great. What is it? Ponder these questions.*

Art can reflect the noblest emotions as well as the trivial aspects of life. Correspondingly the resulting work will have its greater or lesser significance and will exercise an influence upon the world for a longer or shorter span of years. Great art, then, may be defined as that art which deals with the deepest human emotions and appeals to the greatest numbers over the longest period of time.

Americans are sometimes praised, more often criticized, for wanting only the very biggest and the best. Yet with all our wealth and power and bigness in other fields, we have produced in the realm of ideas, in the course of our history, perhaps two or three men — Franklin, Jefferson, who else? — who in allrounded genius can compare in stature to the galaxy of giants which little Florence and little Athens, no bigger than Worcester, Massachusetts, or Kalamazoo, Michigan, actually spawned upon the world.

It is well to pay homage to the great creators of the past, the fixed stars about which for centuries have revolved the lesser lights. But it is also wise to remember that the height of the pyramid is measured by the width of the base. Great artists and thinkers are only found in that civilization which has produced generously on a smaller scale.

I remember in the early New Deal days the controversies that went on in framing the policies of the Section of Painting and Sculpture in the Treasury under Edward Bruce, and that of the Art Section of the Works Progress Administration under the equally brilliant guidance of Holger Cahill. The latter was set up under Harry Hopkins' Relief Program. It was nurtured by the philosophy that during the depression a starving artist deserved the same treatment from our government as the least deserving plumber. The challenge to his critics was that every one of the painters on relief could be usefully employed to make our country a lovelier and a happier place to live in. And he thus proudly justified the expenditure of the taxpayer's money, apart from and in addition to any material or political expediency of relief.

Although open to the most bitter criticism of any of Roosevelt's cultural projects, the accomplishment of Cahill's program was truly immense. At its peak he employed five thousand artists. They worked in easel painting, murals, sculpture, and ceramics. They gathered material for the American Index of Design, that beautiful record of the craft art of our country from Colonial times, which is now housed in our National Gallery and sent on frequent tours to foreign countries. The project also established Community Art Centers in hundreds of our small rural towns, where no art activity had before been seen. And it employed for the first time and kept alive during those lean and hopeless years artists who since then have been on every roster of the Guggenheim Foundation and who now hang their work on our museum walls.

Cahill, in short, with the backing of Hopkins and Roosevelt, who as much as any man I have ever known understood the implication of art in the lives of human beings and in society, gave a forward thrust to the young, anonymous artists of our nation, and to the art-hungry little Main Streets of our vast and sometimes ugly land, which had never before been experienced. That forward thrust has not yet been arrested. The ever-renewed harvest, the seeds of which Cahill and Hopkins and Roosevelt sowed, will be gathered in for many generations. They harrowed the soil for the bonanza crops which one day will fully ripen.

Edward Bruce, who died prematurely in the traces, fighting a losing game against a creeping paralysis, was governed, in his direction of the Section of Painting and Sculpture under the Building Program of the Treasury Department, by a totally different philosophy. Since he was spending the taxpayer's money in the decoration of public buildings, through the allocation of a small percentage of the construction costs, it behooved him to obtain outstanding works of art by the best artists of the country. In building up the Section, the first generous support of mural art by our government, Ned Bruce had every qualification. Himself an artist, he had been a corporation lawyer and a business executive before he took up painting. Back of his painting was a philosophy. He had studied Chinese art in the Orient and the cinquecento in Italy. He was vastly popular with everyone in Washington, and he kept open house. He was a promoter, an idealist, an astute politician and a fury for work. And to him his work was a crusade. He would seem indeed an impossible gift from Heaven to artists and the cause of art. No other at that particular moment could have manipulated the pawns so effectively. He was both a skeptic and a sentimentalist, a skeptic about human beings and a sentimentalist about art and his friends. His taste was catholic. He stood neither to the extreme left nor at the right. His paintings were in museums. All his life he had talked to politicians, lobbyists and the upper brackets of industry. With the backing of Eleanor Roosevelt and Eleanor Morgenthau, who helped him over many a hurdle, he was responsible for the success of the Section.

The difference in his approach from the time-honored caution of every Ministry of Fine Arts for the past five hundred years was that he believed in the selection of young, untried talent from every state in the country through a system of open and juried competitions. Although Bruce insisted that he would only accept the best, while Cahill averred that he

could always profitably employ the worst artists, the two programs —
though frequently at odds with one another and openly clashing in the
heat of the ideologies which so enlivened those glowing New Deal days
— often dove-tailed together in a truly American tradition of decentralized
and democratic handling.

I happened to be a close friend at the time of both Cahill and Bruce,
and had taken some humble part in the organization of the two projects.
I could listen with respect and sympathy to both their points of view. For
I felt that together they represented a well-rounded and complete government art program. I tried once or twice to reconcile their differences. It
was one of my regrets that this was not possible. In the rough-and-tumble
scramble for survival in political Washington, where departmental parti-
sanship and loyalties often cut sharply across mutual interests and ideals,
these two men and their organizations grew further and further apart.
Today both are almost forgotten by a new generation of painters in the
tornado of hurry and fear which sweeps about the world. In the Hall of
Fame of tomorrow American artists should raise a tablet to their memory. They were pioneers who blazed a trail.

In the discussions over the accomplishments and the shortcomings of
the two projects, I often used to say that it boiled down to a debate as to
whether Leonardo and Michelangelo created the fifteenth century or
whether the fifteenth century was necessary to produce a Leonardo. Bruce
was after the Leonardos; Cahill insisted on the need of first creating a
fifteenth century. But one cannot have one without the other. The fixed
stars and the many tiny comets will both help to light the sky.

My definition of great art, as that which deals with the deepest human
emotions and appeals to the greatest number of people over the longest
period of time is, I think, a valid one. And today it is perhaps not a bad
rule of thumb for artists and public to keep somewhere tucked away in
the back of their minds. There is so much going on in the art world that
is intellectual sleight-of-hand; a little petty, a little neurotic; overripe or
corn-meal mush. Not quite simply and deeply felt. The times may have
left our nerves a bit frayed. We need sharp flavoring, relishes and spices,
on our beef and potatoes.

Any definition of great art must, however, be arbitrary and, I believe,
a little confusing. The emphasis on greatness, in our varied, democratic,

decentralized and humanistic tradition, is not nearly so important as is diversity, the challenge of the individual's point of view. If art is imaginative expression, then a work of art has complete beauty when it has complete expression. Complete expression cannot have degrees of beauty. The importance of a work of art is that it is unique. And one can measure the greatness of a civilization by the number of unique ideas to which it can give utterance. As Lord David Cecil points out in his *Art of Reading*, "The fact that any genuine work of art is unique should also discourage us from the seductive practice of ranking writers; drawing up a neat close list . . . with first, seconds and thirds judiciously awarded . . . Critics love dividing literature into categories, distinguishing between major and minor art, primitive art and decadent art, light and serious art, healthy and morbid art. There is no harm in doing this . . . as long as they remember that the only really important distinction is that between good and bad art."

France has a great civilization, not because it has produced, among other men of genius, great writers and painters. That is never enough. Its art history is great because it has turned out many *petits maîtres,* artists in humble spheres, and a high appreciation of such humble art. The smallest creative gift is enough, on condition that it is honestly spoken; but also what prodigious courage, faith and energy are needed to produce that little! The brightness of the sky comes from many tiny stars; never just from the few great ones.

It must be remembered, too, that although only the very greatest periods of civilization produced the giants, it is certainly also true that one can have comparatively important periods of artistic creation with no giants at all. This becomes quite evident when we remember that all the incomparable wealth of the so-called primitive schools — American Indian, Mayan, Tarascan, Polynesian and African — was completely anonymous. The quality that struck many of us as the most exciting in the recent exhibitions of current American painting and the graphic arts at New York's Metropolitan Museum — as in the earlier Artists for Victory Exhibition, also held at the Metropolitan in 1943 — was the very high quality of what I think of as anonymous American art; that is, the jury-selected work of the younger men and women from every state in the country.

I think it can be truly said, in view of this ubiquitous, anonymous art, having distinction, talent, and individuality, that there is a very important art movement in America today; although we may not have produced any artists comparable in stature to the Manets, the Renoirs and Degas; the Van Goghs, Gauguins, and Cézannes; the Picassos, Matisses and Rouaults, who so uniquely characterize the great French movements of the past hundred years.

This admittedly is true. Be it remembered, however, by those few snob collectors and museum directors who in ignorance and in bad taste disparage contemporary American art, that all the outstanding European names that are known today were also known prior to 1915; before World War I. Can you count on one hand those that were not? While if you mention a hundred outstanding American artists — and here again the choice is yours — can you think of any who were known and exhibiting before 1915? And how very few before 1920; and many others that were unheard of ten years ago. America is shaping today in many fields of endeavor unique images of visual perception.

There is a difficulty, too, in grading art. As we know, taste varies from generation to generation. Each new era, even decade, will set new standards of value on the art of the past, and will look for different qualities in the work of contemporaries. The giants of yesterday are the pygmies of today. Vermeer was unknown fifty years after his death. Rembrandt during his lifetime was almost forgotten. El Greco was discovered about 1870. As Van Wyck Brooks observes in his *Makers and Finders*: "Only a handful of writers are perennially 'great,' and every generation selects its own affinities in the past, the writers who are congenial to its own special nature."

All we must look for, then, is a uniqueness, a completeness of expression; the rare, incomparable, eccentric and unmatched. But, alas, there is no way of knowing how we shall value tomorrow this uniqueness of our great men — our Picassos, Rouaults, and Matisses. This is the implication of the statement that a work of art continues to grow after it is created. For surely the continually changing power to influence, educate and control; to set standards; to give delight and evoke sympathy is a quality of communicability which we associate with a living psyche. Some art stays always young. Much of it is in the normal process of slowly dying. But that it has a life of its own, quite apart from that breathed into it by its creator, would seem indisputable.*

It is certainly true that many artists have this feeling about their work. Bernice Kenyon, the poet, told me recently that she felt one must nurture one's creation in the same spirit of sensitive and protective aloofness which the intelligent parent has for her child. And surely this is what Alexis Léger had in mind when he said that "one must only think of the painting and not allow one's participation to interfere with its growth"; what Arnold Schönberg meant in saying that "a work of art must elaborate on its own idea and must follow the conditions which this idea establishes."

I myself have sometimes experienced that sudden feeling of excitement — which so many novelists also mention in the process of their own creative work — when searching for the proper dramatic expression of a face to interpret a mural theme. There was no longer the effort to imagine or to create. Quite suddenly and fortuitously I had actually stumbled across the very individual I was looking for. It was no longer a question of inventing a character, but of hastily transcribing the features of a living man before he should fade from my momentarily focused vision.

All this, of course, may be a fiction of the artist's fancy. But I think it helps us to understand a very important truth. Art and beauty have permanence and reality only so long as they live. And they do not live in the abstract but in the hearts of men. Man has changed little in the past few thousand years. Yet he changes from day to day. Looking at the greatest and most enduring work of art, we see that it too has changed. For is not this its very great significance? Until it dies it is a living thing.

It would follow if this be true that the layman is never in the wrong in merely expressing his like or dislike for even the admittedly greatest

* Marcel Duchamp, in *Modern Artists in America*: "The work of art lives by itself and the artist who happened to make it live is like an irresponsible medium."

Gregory Baleson: "What you are saying . . . implies that, in some sense, the work of art exists before it is there on the canvas."

Duchamp: "Yes, it has to be pulled out."

Darius Milhaud: "And even sometimes, as Mr. Duchamp says — and I agree completely — the work guides you."

Arnold Schönberg: "In the creation of a work of art, nothing should interfere with the idea. A work of art must elaborate on its own idea and must follow the conditions which this idea establishes."

work of art. For he is always the small voice, the tiny fraction of the great body of opinion, which will set the ultimate evaluation on the importance of the unique expression. Who can tell that his dissenting opinion will not forecast the final verdict? He is always in his rights if he declares: "I do not like it. It means nothing to me." He is in fact taking a legitimate esthetic stand. But let him beware of giving his reasons for his aversion. The moment he does so he will put his foot in his mouth. Technical criticism is a matter for the artist or the technical expert, not for the layman. Your position is irrefutable in proclaiming that you do not like spinach. But never say why.

6 ̒

THE ESTHETIC
ENJOYMENT OF ART

From the Author's Diary: October 14, 1952. In Cadiz we visited the Hospital de las Mujeres and sat for a long time before El Greco's Saint Francis. As has happened to me before, when in complete understanding and inbreathing of a great painting, I became aware of a rising flood of energy, exultation and excitement. I felt myself in complete harmony with the majestic rhythms into which the artist had allowed his line to flow. I believed that I was caught in the same wave of ecstacy and satisfaction that the painter himself experienced as he worked. I had the feeling that if I could then have stood by his side and had he looked up at me, we might have nodded to one another, so complete and mutual would have been the shared understanding of his intentions and harmonies. Nicholas Nabokov has described Stravinsky's music as the "artful perception and measurement of the flow of time by means of the most complex and beautiful rhythmic patterns and designs." Yes, that is how the noble orchestration of painting can affect me. I was filled with happiness, a sense of oneness with life, and a momentary conviction that all in our world is well. It is the same feeling, almost one of religious visitation, that I experienced years ago in Paris, when deeply in love.

It has always been recognized that art is a source of pleasure. It has also been taken for granted since the Renaissance that what gives pleasure in works of art is their beauty. It was not until nineteenth-century criticism that it became evident that what was beautiful to one generation or civilization was "gothic" or barbarous to the next. What, then, was the constant element which every age would agree to as beautiful? What in common had the Venus of Milo and an African sculpture, Botticelli's "Spring" and Cubist art? The answer was Clive Bell's "significant form." And form became the substitute for beauty, the apologia of Modernism.

This assumption of form as the source of esthetic pleasure in a work of art would also explain our enjoyment in Raphael's madonnas, and the New Criticism went out of its way to proclaim it. But it must dump overboard such other content in traditional art as seemed to be superfluous to esthetic appreciation: the "lived reality," story, anecdote, fiction, or whatever else you may choose to call it. I have already noted how Ortega bases his whole theory of the necessity of the purification of art by Modernism on his assumption that preoccupation with subject matter excludes esthetic enjoyment: one cannot at the same time concentrate on a lived experience and esthetic form. The elimination of the anecdotal became indeed, in the eyes of the New Criticism, perhaps the most significant contribution of Modern painting.*

Max Eastman had asked in his *Enjoyment of Poetry*: What is it that distinguishes poetry from ordinary language? There can be great poetry without either rhyme or meter but all poetry must have rhythm. All life indeed is charged with rhythm. It is felt in our pulse beat, and occurs in every manifestation of the universe; in the measured ebb and flow of the tides; the waxing and waning of the moon; in the swing of the earth about the sun and in the ordered movements of the constellations. It is seen in the recurrent birth and death of the seasons and is the pattern of procreation and decay in all living things.

So in art there is an ever-present cadence, rhythm, harmony. Some call it unity; others, pattern or form. But it is the integration of this abstract design with some observed fact, or activity, or useful object in life, which gives us esthetic enjoyment. El Greco has painted a face, which I recognize as that of a particular saint or prelate. At the same time I become aware of a pattern, a motif, superimposed upon, integrated with the features; but having an identity as sharp and individual as that of a musical phrase. I enjoy this rhythm in itself as completely as a chord of music.

* "For Modern Art to be born, the art of fiction must die . . . [Painting] is no longer a means of expressing fiction . . . Instead of being a battle horse, a naked woman or whatsoever other anecdote, a painting is essentially a flat surface covered with colors and assembled in a certain order . . . [Modern Art is] the death of fiction."

To outline even more sharply the rift between modern and traditional art Malraux goes further than most critics. He has the boldness to suggest that classic art not only encumbered pure form with the anecdotal but actually called on poetry to express form. For Michelangelo as for Van Eyck "plastic art was the road to a divine abode . . . It is through the medium of poetry that the colors of Leonardo are 'assembled in a certain order'" (André Malraux, in *La Psychologie de l'art*).

10. Titian. *Paul III and His Grandsons.* Naples

11. Piero della Francesca. *Resurrection.* Borgo San Sepolcro

12. Nicholas Poussin. *Triumph of Neptune and Amphitrite*. **Philadelphia** Museum of Art

13. Raphael. *Marriage of the Virgin*. Milan

14. George Biddle. *Caveman's Dream*

15. **Georg Grosz.** *The Agitator.* Mr. and Mrs. Richard S. Davis, Wayzata, Minnesota

16. Bowl with figure of warrior.   Mimbres Valley, New Mexico

17. Bowl.   Zuni Pueblo; New Mexico

But it is the identification of the graphic phrase with the features of a human face which is the chief cause of that peculiar energizing and satisfying concord which we call esthetic pleasure.

Franz Boas, in an essay on the origin of craft design, argues that it had its inception in the abstract pattern created by the rhythmic muscular movement best adapted for the use of a particular tool on a given surface. Anyone who has handled a carpenter's adze, which our forefathers used to dress their timber, a woodcarver's gouge or a stonecutter's point knows how each tool will impose its own individual pattern on wood or stone. This pattern, once developed into a conscious craft design, gives expression to, emphasizes, enhances, and articulates the natural shape of the useful object which it decorates. So in craft art, as in the fine art of painting, it is the integration of this abstract pattern, in this case with a useful object, which gives us esthetic pleasure. And it is equally true that in every art medium — architecture, music, drama, and the dance — it is this integration of a rhythmic design with some aspect of life which gives us art and the fullest esthetic enjoyment.

It would be wrong to suggest that line, color and design, rhythm and form, cannot in themselves give us pleasure. The only question is whether that pleasure is not far greater when we can integrate the abstract pattern with what until then had been merely the formless, haphazard, chaotic, or discordant face of nature.

One can, of course, take pleasure in the lacework tracery of a Moorish tile, of Gothic stone-carving, of seventeenth-century Japanese calligraphy, or of a butterfly's wing, though removed from its proper setting and shut off from the world under glass in a gilded frame on a museum wall. But does it not give us an added and vitalized sense of satisfied participation, when we can identify its music with the inner meaning of some manifestation of life?

This, I would suppose, is the core of the problem which today abstract art must face. I do not think as yet it can be categorically answered one way or the other. There is no doubt that many sincere and thoughtful nonobjective artists believe, not only that their abstractions reflect the hidden meaning of life, but actually offer the art idiom best qualified to give form to the organic expression of our times. Even when abstraction has been used as the vehicle for Dadaist philosophy — the negation of all meaning in life, the protest of the "Big No" — it can be answered that this too is one expression of our period.

Dr. Martin Johnson, the English physicist, suggests in *Art and Scientific Thought* a very interesting analogy between the scientific approach in nuclear physics and the proposed aims of abstract painting. The avant-gardists of Nonobjective Art will find a persuasive and documented justification of their position in his reasoning. He points out that in the sphere of nuclear physics our sense experience of bulk, matter, color, smell, weight, heat and so forth, covers a "real world of electromagnetic forces acting in the almost vacuous spacing of atomic structure." Our knowledge of such structure cannot, however, be predicted by any observation of experiments perceived through the senses; it depends instead on a hypothetical scientific theory or abstraction, which is subject to verification by "its capacity to predict mathematically some experimental result."

Now is it not plausible that today in the field of art, as in the field of science, the sensory observation of the visual aspect of life is not sufficient to reveal the organic meaning of our world? Can this only be done, or more effectively be done, through abstract images? Would this analogy indeed buttress the belief of Sigfried Giedion that the early works of the Cubists, of Braque, Picasso, Mondrian, Miró, and the others forestalled the styles of architecture because they better reflected the changed conditions of our times? Are Modern Art and modern science "attempting to communicate mental images through patterns and structures and forms in the qualitative domain of feeling and in the quantitative domain of measurement respectively?" Can we draw a picture of the world independently of any direct evidence of the senses?

Now the scientific pattern of abstraction is subject to quantitative verification only if the physicist can state it in a communicable form. Has this test of communicability any counterpart in the imaginative arts? In other words, will a work of art, through its abstract imaginary pattern, evoke the same qualitative or emotional response among many different people over a period of time? Is its emotional message communicable? On this rigid test, it seems to me, must depend to a great extent the validity of Nonobjective Art.

In the sphere of music, I think all will agree that the pure pattern of melody, harmony, and counterpoint, apart from being a source of sensuous pleasure, does communicate emotional, imaginative moods identifiable with a lived experience and capable of verification. The lyric sweetness of Mozart, "the most intimately lovable of musicians," and the mathematically ordered passion of Bach evoke a profound and noble vision of our universe, unsurpassed by any phase of art.

Each aspect of nature, however, finds the appropriate art medium best adapted for its imaginative expression. The color of the morning sky, the song of the catbird, the rhythm of sea waves, and the smell of wild honeysuckle do not evoke in us similar and equally intense emotions. Nonobjective painting can, to a limited extent and under certain circumstances, communicate imaginative ideas, capable of verification.

Standing in front of an early Braque abstraction I had just such an experience. It is a little hard to describe. I had the almost positive conviction of what the artist *felt* about life. I was aware of this as clearly as I understand what Chardin or Goya or John Sargent felt when I see one of their pictures. The painting had communicated a distinct emotional response, a state of mind, a human temperament. And I recall as vividly as if it were before my eyes this moment the particular emotion which was evoked in me nearly fifty years ago by Correggio's "Danae" in the Salon Carré of the Louvre or by the "Drunken Silenus" of Rubens in the Alte Pinakothek in Munich; and this long after the color, composition, and details have faded from my memory.

But as regards most contemporary nonobjective painting I can only say: "It is a harmonious or distasteful arrangement. It gives me the sensation of the juxtaposition of lines and colors. Nothing more. No response to a challenge. No identification with an experience. No communication of an idea."

This at any rate is the absolute test of esthetic enjoyment in a work of art: does it communicate an emotion which can be identified with a lived experience?

7'

GREAT ART IS NEVER PURE

From the Author's Diary: March 4, 1952. Later in the afternoon Corrado Cagli turned up with Carlo Levi. Levi impressed me as intelligent and understanding. He looked for a long time at my lithographs, which were framed and hanging on the walls, and then sank slowly into an armchair. Ponderously built, ill-dressed, and with a gray, opaque skin. His powerful, heavy-lidded profile suggested some wise, benevolent, and cynical Roman Emperor.

I told him I had been reading his Orologia. I asked him to what extent it was autobiographic.

"To a great extent," he said. "For me the autobiographic style is the proper one for our times. It has largely superseded the novel, which has become a discarded form."

I told him I had seen his paintings at the Wildenstein Galleries in New York, where I had held a retrospective exhibition of portraits in 1948. He too is interested in portraiture. We both deplored the fact that it most certainly seems today a lost art, too.

I said: "To me the portrait of a face on whose lines are bitten the challenge and response of life has the drama of a three-volume novel."

He said: "It is true. A portrait can be a human tragedy — or comedy at that."

We both condemned the current nonsense, so popular in esthetic art circles, that sentiment has nothing to do with painting; that it lies within the province of poetry and fiction.

I said: "The people who believe this are rationalizing their own lack of feeling for human beings and human nature. It is quite absurd to assume that any one art form has an exclusive jurisdiction to deal with a particular attribute of nature."

We were in full agreement about the sterility of purity in art. The question which I cannot satisfactorily answer is the current craze for purity.

Increasingly during the past hundred years there has been a tendency to eliminate from art, and to disregard as irrelevant, the lived reality which was so dear to nineteenth-century artists. André Malraux even suggests that Manet's portrait of Clémenceau is the *accoucheur* — the midwife — of the whole modern trend in painting, because in the portrait the life of the brush-stroke and of the loaded pigment superseded the character of the sitter.

But here Malraux finds himself in a dilemma. With his profound historical sense he is aware of the absolute continuity of art, the strand which links the successive and overlapping cultures of the world. And he fully realizes that in the art of the past the human element — life, nature, character, and the anecdotal — was essential. Yet, he argues, the essence of Modern Art is its purification of the anecdotal. "Pour que l'art moderne naisse, il faut que l'art de la fiction finisse." It is the paint that gives us esthetic pleasure; that has the wallop. Never the story, the literary fiction.

It is here that he has been trapped by the fallacy that has clouded critical thinking for the past fifty years. No great art is pure, nor is there any thinkable reason why it should be. And this is of course eminently true of the great schools of abstract painting and sculpture which have flourished many centuries before the birth of Modernism. The highly sophisticated abstract art of the Hopi Indians, of the primitive tribes of the upper reaches of the Amazon, are charged with religious symbolism. The jades of the Han dynasties of China were to be fingered as well as looked at; and they had, too, a philosophic significance.* In fact, in the greatest Chinese art the poetic or philosophic content is always as relevant in the imaginative expression as is the visual image. For over a thousand years the highly intricate abstract patterns that were the only permitted idiom for Islamic painting and sculpture had the twin functions

---

* "But the status of these little carvings was enhanced by a uniquely Chinese addition to the visual esthetic judgment — the appreciation of tactile and auditory values in an artist's material. Whether the jade was the oily nephrite or the icy jadeite, to handle and feel the surface texture of a vessel or figure, and to hear the sonority of a suspended disc or plate, always reinforced the affectionate reverence which the stone seems to have aroused throughout Chinese history . . . [They felt] that even trivial objects, if beautiful, can exert a far-reaching effect upon the maker's and beholder's attitude to larger matters. They saw that even the lesser arts and the very minor graces of life may have profound results in the decisions of the practical man by the orientation of his mind that they compel . . . [When this is understood] the western mind will have mastered the East by capturing its most intimate treasure. The age-long antithesis between the visionary and the useful will then have been resolved into the true superman, logician, mystic and practical man at once." — Martin Johnson, on Chinese jade in *Art and Scientific Thought*.

of the decoration of architectural surfaces and the interpretation through symbols of religious dogma. And it would be quite untenable to disassociate the music of Bach and Mozart, the most abstract of musicians, from the motivating purposes — the dance, song, requiem, mass or opera — for which they were intentionally composed.

If it is argued that subject matter and the human incident is foreign to the esthetic intent of modern painting and sculpture, what then must we say of some of the completely traditional art of Picasso, Lipchitz, Noguchi, Stuart Davis and others? For they would be the last to admit that such work is without esthetic significance. Nor, in discussing the Modern Movement is it either logical or wise to isolate the visual arts from such other art forms as the ballet, opera, drama, or even music. Arnold Schönberg, whose twelve-tone scale is a cornerstone of ultra-modern music, wrote many of his compositions to accompany dramatic recitatives and his works are as moodily sentimental as are Kafka's novels. Is the "story" an esthetic defect or irrelevant in Joyce's *Ulysses,* and in Gertrude Stein's *Three Lives, Ten Portraits* or *Tender Buttons?*

Such a line of thinking is patently nonsense. All must agree that in the past — and in many other fields of art today — there is no such thing as purity of art form or the necessary disassociation of one art form from another. The fact that many artists have returned to the abstract idiom, as they so often have in the past, does not argue for the purity of that expression. Most of these artists are convinced that their works also carry ulterior philosophic significance, or indeed may be combined with the other art forms effectively.*

Every imaginative response to life will find its appropriate art form. Certain of these are highly abstract and others realistic and more easily identifiable with the visual world and human nature; while in still other cases a union of various art forms — music, poetry, painting, drama, and the dance — seems needed to express the most imaginative response to certain aspects of life. The degree of abstraction or of realism, of purity or of synthesis with other art forms, is in itself of no importance. The only significance of any idiom is its relevancy and fitness for one particular

* As when Fernand Léger and George Antheil collaborated in the twenties in the production of the *Ballet Méchanique.*

imaginative expression of life. For an art idiom is a language, a means of communication, with no inherent esthetic value other than the use to which it is put; although it is indisputably true that certain art forms have a greater range of communication than others.

It has sometimes been said that the opera is a *bastard* form of art. The metaphor is a most inappropriate one. What is meant is that many nineteenth-century operas are less satisfying than either concert music or drama. The indictment should have been leveled at the particular offspring rather than at mixed parenthood as such.

Primitive art at the dawn of history was intended to serve a strictly utilitarian purpose. The earliest picture-making was an effort by primitive man to impose his will on nature, to slay a buffalo, bring about a fruitful crop, or beget a child by his wife, by painting the animal on the walls of a cave or modeling the symbol of fertility. So art performed a useful service and throughout its great periods it has continued to do so: in oriental and Egyptian art, in Gothic sculpture, in Byzantine church mosaics, and in the murals and portraits of the cinquecento. And it has always seemed to me that, although the ultimate value of art is both its sensuous enjoyment and its reflection and revaluation of life, yet the attempt to divorce it from its utilitarian function by concentrating solely on its esthetic qualities is unfortunate. For it tends to emasculate it by robbing it of its relation to life; just as in contemporary nonobjective painting there is the inherent danger of emasculating it by robbing it of an obvious kinship with experienced reality.

When art performs a utilitarian function by telling a story — as with medieval illuminations, illustrations, cartoons, murals and portraits — the story is as subject to artistic handling as is the painting. There is a mixed parenthood and one cannot be divorced from the other. The mixture is not, of course, in equal proportion. As in the opera music is the dominant element, so in painting, line, color and design shoulder the greater weight in the total impact. But not only the story cannot be dismissed as unessential, its treatment should receive consideration as a legitimate part of the over-all pattern. I would affirm that among the world's great portraits — that terrifying family group of Paul III and his *nipoti* in Naples' Pinacoteca; the equestrian portrait of Charles V in the Prado in Madrid, perhaps the supreme homage to nobility and lordship; and the many profound and tender self-revelations by Rembrandt — the penetration into the shadowy depths of human nature, the intuition of evil, wisdom, brooding sadness, innocence or regret which life's branding-iron has stamped on human faces are as much the appropriate material for the artist to weave into his rhythmic pattern as are his line, color and design.

What is objectionable in the bad academic painting of the past century is not the presence of subject matter or fiction, but the inartistic manner in which it was handled; the crude realism and the lack of pattern, selection and dramatic unity. There is more incident and melodrama in Bosch's pictures than were ever in Madame Tussaud's Chamber of Horrors in Baker Street. In Carpaccio's "The Legend of Saint Ursula" there is more sentiment and anecdote than in any of Norman Rockwell's covers for *The Saturday Evening Post*. In Bouguereau and the English Royal Academicians there was never too much sweetness, innocence and sensibility — for Simone Martini and Filippo Lippi and Sandro Botticelli were incomparably more sweet. It is the bathos, vulgarity and bad painting and drawing of these academicians which are at fault.

There is never too much story, but the story as well as the painting must have scale and design. And this means its proper subordination to the unity of the whole. If human psychology and the story are the proper theme for literary treatment, they are also a possible element that can be woven into the over-all structure of painting and sculpture. Whether artists today are interested in life and human beings is another question. But once and for all let us bury the meaningless cliché that art need be pure; or painting divorced from incident, anecdote, drama or the portrayal of man's soul.

Part II ⋅ Victory or Defeat of Modernism?

8 ˊ

MODERNISM: THE MIND
OR THE EYE

From the Author's Diary: January 26, 1952. Called with Hélène on Lionello Venturi, to whom Ambassador Tarchiani had given me a letter. In the overcrowded little apartment at 42 Corso Trieste — in one of the many "Bronxes" on the fringe of old Rome — the walls are stacked high with books. The quiet, comfortable, middle-class atmosphere of the dedicated European scholar. Venturi had been suffering from a long bout of rheumatism. He lay on a couch, wrapped in a woolen shawl, while Signora Venturi poured tea and helped us to the many strange little sweetmeats which accompany the continental ritual. Venturi is a large man, ponderous, slow-moving, benign and imposing. His kindly, intelligent eyes were blurred and seemed quite thrown out of focus by the strong lenses of his eyeglasses. This contributed to the effect of a gentle and scholarly bullfrog. What he sees through his glasses is a mystery. When he looked at my lithographs, he held them an inch or two from his eyes. But I believe he liked them. He commented on their strength and asked me if I should care to show them at the exhibition of "The Demoniacal in Art," which is shortly to be held at the Palazzo Barberini. (See Fig. 14.)

We talked for an hour on the many striking similarities between Byzantine and Modern Art. For one thing he believes that the Byzantine mosaic muralists conceived of their effects primarily in color; that they proceeded from color to plastic form. And this is substantially true of much contemporary painting. He believes, as I do, that the architectonic powers of Byzantine and trecento art was subsequently weakened by the preoccupation of the Renaissance painters with perspective, anatomy, and the location of the human figure against the backdrop of nature; with the vanishing point on the horizon line, an approach so dear to Piero, Verrocchio, Mantegna, Leonardo, and the others. What a tremendous opportunity for architectural scale, when man is conceived in the framework of hierarchic or systematized ideas! In connection with all of this I asked him what had been his impression of the Mexican murals. Curiously enough he does not seem to take them too seriously. How

few Europeans understand their importance! They judge them by the narrow
parochial standards of the intelligentsia of the Ecole de Paris.

I asked him to what extent John Dewey had been influenced by Croce.
He said that Dewey denied it but admitted that he had been influenced by
current European thought.

"Had Croce been influenced by James; for undoubtedly Dewey had?"

"Not at all."

"And what were Croce's most important works on esthetics?"

"You must read two of them. Di Poesia is the greatest and the most im-
portant. But its proper understanding rests most solidly on the more complete
philosophic expression in his Estetica."

Before leaving he autographed for us a copy of his book, Pour comprendre
la peinture. *He promised to visit us upon our return from skiing in the Dolo-*
mites, when he felt he would be fully recovered.

The significance of Modern Art can only be appreciated if we think
of it in the wider context of world trends, as an idiom or expression of a
critical historical period in the history of Western civilization. One such
major curve of history has been appropriately named by historians the
Age of Faith. The Middle Ages were by no means a dark and recessive
interlude between Roman-Hellenic civilization and the Modern World,
but a well-rounded and universal period of history, with its own clear-cut
intuitive expression of life. That civilization expressed its belief in man's
original sinfulness here below, as in the reward of another life through
repentance and faith, in revealed truth and the identity of religion, science, and philosophy. If any one man created a period, the Emperor Con-
stantine created the Middle Ages; not so much by the formal recognition
of Christianity, as by the marriage of Greek philosophy to oriental mysticism and absolutism, which was the character he stamped upon it when
he moved the center of Western civilization from Rome to the Bosphor-
ous. Roman-Hellenic culture was slowly disintegrating in Europe. It remained frozen for a thousand years in the monolithic traditionalism of
the East. The Byzantine Empire lasted from 323 until 1453, when it was
destroyed by the Turks. Its life span was three times that of the Roman
world empire. For a millennium its philosophy and art permeated and
deeply influenced European civilization.

Medieval art, unquestionably influenced by Byzantine traditionalism,
reveals medieval man as an integral part of a universal and hierarchic

structure. His stature, location, intention and significance are in relation to a philosophic concept, absolute, eternal and fixed. And this unquestioned faith is given expression in every form of art: in Dante's *Divine Comedy*, in the "Crucifixion" of Cimabue in the Uffizi Gallery of Florence, in the mosaics of Monreale at Palermo or in the Basilica of St. Apollinare in Classe at Ravenna, in the twelfth-century sculpture on the West Portal of Chartres Cathedral, as indeed in every cathedral of medieval Europe. God, the Virgin, angels, prophets, man, sheep, fish, lion and eagle have each their appropriate, revealed and ordained scale and meaning. The cathedral spire binds the world to Heaven. Every aspect of life declares a unity, faith and permanence.

Another such major historical cycle is the Modern World, ushered in by the Italian Renaissance. The latter has been called the Age of Man and also the Age of Science. Today in the fields of art and philosophy the scientific and the humanistic approach may not seem consonant with each other. Perhaps diametrically opposed. Yet in their twin assault on the medieval mind, humanism and science stood bravely for the same objectives. For the Renaissance questioned the assurance that man should stake all his hopes on a celestial paradise, and believed more firmly that he could install through science, reason and enlightenment his own paradise here below. So the study of nature — science — and the study of man — humanism — were the dual expressions of an identical faith. And in the art of the Renaissance, as in the art of the next five centuries, man is conceived and proportioned, not so much with reference to any absolute cosmogony or concept — the deity, Mary, the seraphim or eternal life — but in reference to nature, as he is seen in life, with the eyes, not with the mind.* (See Figs. 10, 12, 13, 19.)

* "During the Middle Ages . . . the artist's starting-off point was an abstract model, supplied to him by tradition, and this, in order to become a work of art, had to be transformed into a concrete portrayal inspired by mystical emotions he personally experienced . . . During the XIIIth and XIVth centuries the Italians kept to this progression from the abstract to the concrete, which had been that of the Middle Ages . . . For all the compelling sense of reality he imparted to his art, we find this even in Giotto. But from Masaccio, the painter obviously starts out from an observation of nature in terms of structure and perspective (from concrete reality in other words), and only then allows his creative imagination to take its flight into the loftiest realms of abstraction. The scientific analysis of optical experience which began in Florence in the first part of the XVth century influenced the whole aspect of painting for many centuries — until round about 1900, to be precise, at which times we see signs of a revival of abstract art . . . Beginning from the early years of our century, a need has been felt to reinstate the ab-

Herein, in painting as in sculpture, lies the whole significance of the introduction of Euclidian perspective and anatomical study by the *quattrocento* artists. Nineteenth-century scientific criticism erroneously assumed that perspective, the use of the vanishing point, and correct anatomical study were a technical advance over the ignorance of medieval art. It is true that neither would have been possible without the new learning and observation of nature, ushered in by the Renaissance. But until recently it has been overlooked that what art gained by perspective and anatomy in approximation to visual accuracy was lost in ideal truth. For nature presents us with many conflicting truths and art must select and reject from the ideas and material at its disposal. In medieval art, as in almost all great art until the Renaissance, there is an arbitrary stylization of this material. Japanese artists, for instance, spread a black wash across the top of the print to suggest the night. In Byzantine mosaics the color of a robe identified a saint. In *trecento* murals human figures are drawn on a constant scale with reference to each other. But God, the Virgin and the angels are on a different scale. And this perspective — "the relative importance and presentation of facts from a special point of view" — which is of the mind, is surely as intelligent as that other perspective of the eye, which sees figures larger or smaller only in reference to the horizon line.

This latter Euclidian perspective indeed would be a mere technical triviality, the meaningless visual distortion of a truth known to the mind, if it were not a symbol of the whole new approach of the *quattrocento* toward nature and man. The Renaissance for the first time envisaged man not as a link in a systematized universe but against the framework of his natural background, as belonging to and part of nature.

Arbitrary or stylized perspective, drawing and color are characteristic, however, of the greatest art periods, of early Greek and sixteenth-century Persian art, of the Byzantine and Gothic, of Chinese and Japanese and Cambodian. During these periods the meaning of a line was considered more weighty than anatomical exactness. The organic or symbolic significance of color was held more important than its fleeting mood. The

stract as a source of inspiration — whether abstract forms and geometrical space, or the unknown, the unseen, the super-real. Is this the revival of an age-old craving for God, or, rather, the Irrational knocking at the door of our hearts?" (Lionello Venturi, in *Italian Painting*.)

intention of perspective was to indicate enduring rather than transitory and inconsequential relations. For in these periods when art reached the heights, there was a balance between mental and visual truth—things seen by the mind as well as by the eye.

The Renaissance and the Modern World have also created art on this high level. At given moments in the past five hundred years there has been this appropriate balance between the curiosity in our human world and a preoccupation with the search for the absolutes; between the experience of lived reality and formal expression. For it would seem that this proper balance is necessary to reflect the deeper human emotions; to appeal to the greatest numbers over the longest period of time. And undoubtedly in the field of painting much of Impressionism was art on this high level.

French Impressionism was the last chapter in this long art cycle between Masaccio's frescoes for the Brancacci Chapel in Florence and the birth of Modern Art. It was the final revolt against formalism: traditional composition and drawing, studio lighting, and the bathos of official art. Not the grouping of figures in a painting to produce a dramatic or formal composition, but the "candid camera" informality of life. Not the graphic delineation which indicates form and what is apperceived by the mind—the line of Leonardo and Michelangelo and Raphael; but the presentation without critical comment of what is *seen* with the eye. In fact, not objects at all, for we do not *see* objects. The retina of the eye catches patches of color and light. It is the *mind* that identifies these colors through experience. This approach is not true of all Impressionistic art. It does not hold for Degas, or Toulouse-Lautrec, or much of Renoir. But it is essentially true of the technical contribution of Impressionism to Western Art. And one can properly say that in this sense Impressionism is the final logical step, if not the *reductio ad absurdum,* of the scientific approach in art; for it has completely divorced the mind from the eye.

With the Post-Impressionists—Cézanne, Van Gogh, and Gauguin—the pendulum had started to swing back toward the traditional formalism of Renaissance art, but also toward the Renaissance preoccupation with and love of nature and life. Cézanne's painting is often awkward and confused, but on this score his writing is unclouded: "The Louvre is a good book to consult; but it should only be a mediator. The real and prodigious work to undertake is the diversity of the face of nature." And again: "But I must always come back to this: the painter must dedicate himself entirely to the study of nature." And again: "The Louvre is the book in which we learn to read. But we must not satisfy ourselves with the handsome formulas of our illustrious predecessors. We must abandon them to study the beauties of nature."

The Master of Aix died in 1906. He has been called the forerunner of the Modern Movement. He was most certainly not its prophet. Nor could he ever have been its happy apologist. He would have preferred inclusion in the Pantheon of the great humanists and traditionalists of the past. And perhaps history will evaluate his genius as having put a period to a long cycle of European painting, rather than as having initiated a new age.

There has been, then, a long span in Western art which placed an insistence on the eye as well as on the mind. It stressed the importance of the outward-looking, extroverted, objective vision of the world in the swing away from the introverted, inward-searching, self-revelation of Gothic and Byzantine art. But had not the movement reached a dead end with the extreme innovations of Impressionism, whose protagonists held that in art there is no place for the mind at all? What matters is the way the eye sees things — at ten o'clock in the morning, at high noon or against the setting sun.

Post-Impressionism had attempted to reconcile Renaissance formalism with the technical innovations of Impressionism. But with Modernism came no reconciliation with the preceding realism; there came instead an abrupt swing back to the philosophical tenets of Byzantine art.

Only thus can we understand so much of Modern painting that troubled its critics forty years ago: the denial of Euclidian perspective and the preoccupation with "atmosphere," which Bernard Berenson notes as one of the major contributions of the Renaissance; the use of color organically, rather than with reference to optical laws or the transitory moods of nature; the return to abstraction, which Lionello Venturi believes to be so characteristic of Byzantine and trecento art; and the obsession of modern painters that ideas and symbols are more important than mere visual truth. And this, too, explains how the early modern artists could have been affected at once by such apparently disparate influences as the Italian Primitives, African, Gothic, Polynesian and Mayan. For have not all these art expressions and the cultures to which they belonged placed the emphasis on introverted and self-revealed knowledge rather than on the outward-looking, extroverted and objective vision of life — on the mind rather than on the eye?

9'

MODERNISM: A NEW
STYLE IN DESIGN

*From the Author's Diary: April 4, 1949. I saw the superb, retro-
spective exhibition of Braque at the Museum of Modern Art. It confirms
what Albert Gleizes told me in Paris in 1923. He spoke of the intellectual
ferment going on there in 1907, 1908, and 1909. It was influenced to a great
extent by Cézanne's later work, which burst spontaneously into Cubism.
Braque's painting, seen in its totality, strengthens the belief which I have
always entertained: that the twin horns of Modern Art were a preoccupation
with the elements of design and at the same time a metaphysical inquiry into
the relation between representation and pure form in painting. One can
almost say, looking at these paintings, that abstraction reached its culmination — and its dead end — by 1912.
But for me, the beautiful Degas retrospective at Wildenstein's.*

*Rome, October 24, 1951. One can admire the baroque, though it is not
to my taste; nor, I fancy, to the taste of our age. The absolute vulgarity of the
"interior decoration" of Saint Peter's displays the baroque at its most pre-
tentious, ornate and nouveau-riche. Was it not largely paid for indeed by the
gold of the Incas? One almost feels that the center of Christianity was
modeled on the Waldorf-Astoria. Even Michelangelo's "Last Judgment"
writhes and squirms. Brancusi and Fernand Léger probably would say that
it is the precursor of the current macaroni-spaghetti style. And yet Michelangelo, as El Greco, is the baroque at its most sublime. But how one longs
in this style for the right angle, horizontal and perpendicular. That is how
Modern Design has conditioned us. Who can say that it is not a sweeping
reform? Only the Chinese, at their best, could achieve strength without the
use of angles and straight lines.*

A little over forty years ago there was no Modern Design. Twenty-
five years ago it was very generally accepted all over the world. It is hard

for us to realize, now that it is all over, the enormous change in the visual pattern of our lives brought about in less than two decades by the acceptance of this new style in design. This change of the visual pattern in our cultural life has been as radical and far-reaching as for instance the change in our economic life, brought about by the introduction of the automobile. It is hard for us, too, to recapture the vehemence, intransigence, and energy — "the sound and the fury" — that ushered in the new movement. Artists and critics still argue about the avant-gardist trends of Modern Art. But there is quite a difference between the suave, urbane and cultured symposia of middle-aged and successful radicals, tape-recorded at the "Artist Sessions at Studio 35" or at the Museum of Modern Art in New York and the noisy, ill-bred and turbulent violence to which one listened with delight in the smoke-filled atmosphere of the Dôme or Rotonde. It is a little hard to beat the tom-toms once you are on the winning side. Modern Design has been firmly in the saddle — of hoi polloi as of the upper crust — for over a generation.

The arguments were not always clearly stated. Art students and young painters are not as articulate as middle-aged intellectuals. But they knew how to voice their emotions. I recall two instances.

One spring evening in 1923 Moïse Kisling, who — believe it or not — was a Modern, sat outside the Dôme with a group of friends, Jules Pascin, Kogan, Marie Vassiliev, Chana Orloff, Larionov and others. A critic, with whom he had had some esthetic altercation, approached the group, delivered a short and angry harangue and hurled his missile, wrapped in a copy of *Paris-Soir*, at Kisling's head. It was horse manure. For the evening Moïse was the standard-bearer of the new faith.

During the winter of 1924 I gave a party in my studio at 84 Rue d'Assas. It was a mixed crowd. Chagall was there, Guy Arnoux, Orloff, Hunt Diederich, Marsden Hartley, Fernand Léger and Pascin. Louis Ritman, whom I had known in Giverny in 1915 and 1916, brought his friend Chaim Soutine. From the beginning I sensed a certain tension among the guests. Hunt Diederich's beautiful wife Wanda sat down on Marsden's palette, which did not improve her dress or her temper. Soutine, pale, crumpled and a little forbidding, asked me in a tense voice where were the pornographic drawings, was this or was it not a *maison de passe*, and when would the girls undress and the floor show begin. At first I took this for his dry Latin Quarter humor and I wrote it off on my drinks. Louis seemed much disturbed. Things did not seem to jell. Léger looked ruffled and left early. I was told the next day by some of my friends that Soutine was furious because Léger had been invited. They disapproved of each other's painting.

It was this spirit, contumacious, alive and vehement, among the young painters from many nations gathered together in Paris in the early years before the First World War which created Modern Design.

The movement was a swing of the pendulum away from the formless realism of Impressionism.* It was essentially a preoccupation with form and design. This search for form gradually split into two different trends. Yet esthetically these two currents had nothing to do with each other. I believe that this has never been clearly understood and never before been said. The first was a reaction against the neobaroque, neoclassic, neo-Renaissance and Victorian design, which in various styles had dominated Europe since the cinquecento. The second was a new esthetic philosophy — reflecting most assuredly the spiritual emptiness and chaos of the period and the defeatism of the generation of Marcel Proust, James Joyce, Franz Kafka and T. S. Eliot — but also in quest of a new meaning to life. This philosophy asserted that the artist is hindered in his effort to create pure form by the literal transcription or interpretation of nature; and consequently that he can best give expression to his imaginative vision through the abstract. Ortega's "dehumanization" is the expression of the disillusion with the present and the past. Giedion and Gleizes, a fine artist himself and the theoretic exponent of Cubism and abstract art, see in abstract art the "outward visible sign" of a New World.†

Modern Design must not be confused with the Modern Movement. The Modern Movement is a new approach to life, a different world

* "The naturalistic school has put forward the following definition of a work of art: *The work of art is nature seen through a temperament* . . . I shall completely reverse this naturalistic formula: *The work of art is a temperament which manifests itself through nature's laws*" (Albert Gleizes, in *La Mission creatrice de l'homme*).

† "The period for copying [nature] has passed; that of interpreting [nature], without other guidance than taste, has also passed . . . Each artist will know that he must express in his work the harmonies which he divines on a spiritual plane; . . . through the Unity of those general laws which give the Universe its splendid homogeneity" (Gleizes, *La Mission creatrice de l'homme*).

philosophy, the revaluation of basic values; just as the Middle Ages and the Renaissance involved altered feelings and attitudes toward life, based on new faiths and new ethical standards.

Modern Art is the intuitive, imaginative expression of our Modern World. It is good, bad or indifferent art, individual, anonymous or academic. But if it has a meaning at all, it is that particular art which is an expression of the modern spirit. It is not just the art created by contemporary men. Modern Art is an explosion, a discharge, a message, vision, belief, expression.

Modern Design is the vessel containing the message: the rifled barrel directing the explosive force. It is a graphic idiom, a style, which can be broken down into specific elements, recognizable at a glance. It is a pictorial channel of communication. Like every style, it is that particular language which living creative artists have found most appropriate to convey their expressive reaction to life.

In every field of art the Modern Movement has created or attempted to create its appropriate style. Sometimes successfully and easily acceptable. Sometimes less successfully. Then it may seem a false start. The success and easy acceptance of the style depends to a great extent on its ability to deal with basic human needs and communicate its message to the greatest numbers. In music Schönberg, Hindemith and Charles Edward Ives have been wrestling with new idioms of expression in the creation of the twelve-note scale and of atonal and polytonal harmonies — music not written in any one mode or written, as also by Ives, concurrently in different musical keys.*

Musical critics may not all agree that these attempts have been successful; or that they are needed to express the content of Modernism. I remember, in a symposium on contemporary art at Duke University several years ago, Roger Huntington Sessions saying that more combinations of notes, formerly considered a dissonance, have been accepted as a

---

* Marion Tyler Chase tells me this charming anecdote, which she had in connection with a performance of the Ives Second Symphony in Danbury, where he wrote it more than fifty years before. His father, George E. Ives, who at the age of sixteen had been bandmaster of the Brigade Band of the First Connecticut Heavy Artillery — according to President Lincoln the best band in the Union Army — was something of a martinet in the musical education of his son. He used to make young Charles play a tune on the piano in one key and sing it in another. "But why should I do that, Father?" Tapping him gently on the head: "It's to stretch our ears, son; to stretch our ears."

concord during the past fifty years than in the preceding five hundred; and that the layman has not had the necessary time to accustom
himself to these new tonal relations. This same criticism can be made in
other fields. Technical innovations have been made by artists faster than
we have been able to readjust to them. We have not yet geared our ear
or eye to the new "sensibility" which is demanded of us. All musicians
would agree, however, that contemporary music is searching for a vehicle
into which it can pour the content of the Modern World. And in certain
fields contemporary music seems to have succeeded.

In the field of graphic and plastic art, however, Modern Design is
universally accepted, as a mode, a fashion, a style. The Lever Building,
by Skidmore, Owings and Merrill, on Park Avenue in New York; the
design by Raymond Loewy on a package of Lucky Strike cigarettes; the
streamlining, good or bad, of our automobiles and railroad coaches; designs for fabrics, neckties and chinaware; the *New Yorker* cartoons of
Saul Steinberg, Peter Arno and Ludwig Bemelmans — all point to the
obvious fact that for at least a generation, from Hollywood to Rio de Janeiro, from Finland to Tokyo, Modern Design has swept victoriously
around the world. It is a permanent, vital, organic expression of the needs
and aspirations of our new age.

What are the graphic elements, which, when assembled according
to certain general patterns, are "recognizable at a glance" as constituting
the style of Modern Design? I shall try to analyze these elements in the
next chapter.

IO'

GRAPHIC ELEMENTS OF DESIGN

From the Author's Tahitian Diary, May 15, 1920. Listening, during church, to the rhythmic beat of the native singing, I let my mind wander. Recently I have become deeply absorbed in the effort to conventionalize nature and through these abstractions to give new interpretations to every aspect of the landscape. Should not each tree, a wave, a mountain have its own particular symbol, charged with meaning? Assuming that painting is the interpretation of nature in color, line and design, must not the weighted leaf of the banana be presented by a different symbol than the one used for the frightening and feathered palm tree, or the shadowed and royal grandeur of the mango? Such symbolization — or abstraction — of nature was used by the Egyptians, the Chinese, the North American Indians and the creators of French Gothic. And is it not curious that the same graphic elements of design which the Polynesians and the Pueblo Indians used in their mystic symbols are also found in early Greek vase painting?

Church was over. At Tauire Tane's bungalow we lunched on varo, *sea centipede,* ia ota, *raw fish, and suckling pig.*

What do I mean by graphic elements of design? They are the essential component parts, which cannot further be broken down, of a complex graphic structure. Beethoven's Fifth Symphony and a sailor's chanty can both be reduced to the twelve half-tones of the scale. An Islamic arabesque, a drawing of Leonardo or a child's scribble can be boiled down to even fewer essential elements of design. These elements are the dot, the straight line, the circle or segment of a circle, and the ellipse. They are united through alternation, repetition, variation; in parallel relations; in circular symmetry, in axial symmetry, and so on. There are no further elements or possible combinations of elements of any known style in linear design. The basic elements of linear design may be combined with value tones — white to gray to black — or with color, in order to achieve the full range of graphic design.

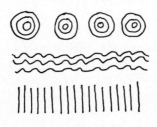

Alternation

Repetition

Parallel Relations

Circular Symmetry

Axial Symmetry

Axial Alternation

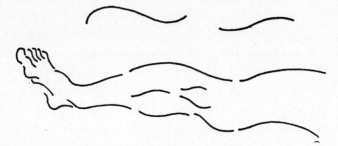

Reverse Curve or "Line of Beauty"

Variation

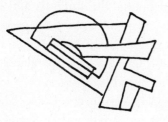 

Asymmetry

While still very young I had felt the charm of the subtle counterpoint rhythms and fugues of line, tone and color in my beloved Japanese prints. At college I slept with a Kiyonaga hanging at the foot of my bed, and I had always been frustrated by the knowledge that I should never own a Sharaku. Three, or at most five, dollars was all that I could then afford for one of these little masterpieces. I had observed how Shunsho or Utamaro could balance the intricacy of many fine lines, or the swaying grace of little Kintoki's demented mother with one heavy splash of black. I had noticed how the earth reds and dull greens and mustard yellows of Hokusai would swing the orchestration of his arabesques back into the center of the print; and how, by covering up with my forefinger the elegant calligraphy of Hiroshige's signature in the lower left-hand corner, I could topple the whole structure of his pale rose landscapes off balance.

I could deliciously let myself go to this feeling of being gently pulled in a dozen directions by line, tone, and color, and also by dramatic incident, yet knowing that so perfect was the artist's adjustment of all these sources of energy that I should never fall.

Music, like painting or formal design, has its own basic elements or syllables, and a systematized grammar governing their use. Musical notes can be arranged into intervals and scales. The notes have vibrations which are subject to exact quantitative measurement. To the average ear certain combinations of notes are in themselves physically satisfying. Other combinations hurt our nerves. The explanation of such satisfaction or distress lies properly in the field of psychology; and the relation between the vibrations corresponding to the musical notes — the intervals and scales — in the realm of physics. Thus in music a quantitative measurement is possible of a physical phenomenon causing an emotion. In other words the grammar of music can be systematized; and the logically related parts of the system are subject to exact mathematical comparison.

Are the elements of the grammar of painting subject to a similar quantitative analysis? Color vibrations can be measured and compared; but color relations do not communicate the same physical reaction of pleasure or distress to the average man, as is the case with sounds. There is one exception. The "warm" colors of the spectrum — yellow, orange and red — evoke physical sensations of warmth, excitement and nearness. The "cool" colors of the spectrum evoke sensations of coolness, serenity, and distance.

And how about the elements of lineal design — dots, lines, segments of circles, and ellipses? Lines cannot be systematized through vibrations, subject to exact quantitative measurement, as is the case with colors and sounds. They may be systematized, however, according to their directions and relations; and these modes — if we may borrow another musical term — do evoke identical physical responses in the average man. Horizontal lines: passivity, weight, repose. Vertical lines: a feeling of upward movement, excitement, physical or spiritual elation. Converging lines or masses: stability, static equilibrium, sustained tension, centripetal energy. Diverging lines or masses: fission, disruption, explosion, centrifugal energy.

There is another interesting analogy — and difference — between formal design and music. That many-sided genius, Jean Jacques Rousseau, in his *Discours sur les sciences et les arts* (1750) called attention to the fact that painting is the only art the esthetic apperception of which is instantaneous. A painting has no beginning, or end, or duration in time. Yet today we speak of the movement of lines; and we criticize a composition as being static or too "busy." The movement of formal design, however, is dependent on physical direction and not on time. Its limitation and uniqueness lies in the fact that its movement is frozen into an instant of infinite duration. It is this frozen music — and the evocation of mood, which its arrested movement creates — that John Keats had in mind in the beautiful "Ode on a Grecian Urn."

> Heard melodies are sweet, but those unheard
> Are sweeter; therefore, ye soft pipes, play on;
> Not to the sensual ear, but, more endeared,
> Pipe to the spirit ditties of no tone:
> Fair youth, beneath the trees, thou canst not leave
> Thy song, nor ever can those trees be bare;
> Bold Lover, never, never canst thou kiss,
> Though winning near the goal — yet, do not grieve;
> She cannot fade, though thou hast not thy bliss,
> For ever wilt thou love, and she be fair!

I I ˒

TWO STYLES IN DESIGN
THROUGHOUT THE AGES

*From the Author's Diary, January 25, 1953. Bernard Berenson has
known both the Steins intimately and was devoted to Leo, who had been his
neighbor in Florence for many years. We talked about them more than once
at "I Tatti." I, too, had a fondness for the one as much as I disliked the other.
Berenson once wrote me: "Leo was persistent, devoted, unambitious, quite
deaf mentally as well as physiologically, a great bore, and something of a
saint . . . In fifty and more years of familiar contact, I never heard him say
a thing that interested me. Yet I loved him and stood him. It took patience."*

*What makes Berenson's mind so delightfully stimulating is that it never
gets the best of his heart; for a great mind must love, hate and have its occasional prejudices and blind spots. A mind without bias and predilections is a
little like a tree without rocks to which its roots can cling. With all her intelligence I, too, used to feel that Gertrude was an "odious and self-admiring"
casuist. On the other hand, Leo was always the earnest and scrupulous inves-
tigator of ultimate truth, although at times his mind was as sprightly and ten-
acious as that of a dung beetle. Once in a while in his Appreciation he has
something important to say. Speaking of the art world of Paris of the twenties:
"At no previous time was so much extravagance admissible and such eccen-
tricity permissible. We are in so many ways at the breakdown of a civilization
of old and established standing, and so vaguely in view of what is to succeed
it, that the future is any man's guess. Therefore one can choose one's costume
and do as one pleases."*

*Leo Stein instinctively felt that the world is standing at the crossroads and
the sign posts are blurred. I remember, too, Ben Shahn saying to me eight or
ten years ago: "Artists react differently to the many aspects of contemporary
life. Only the future can tell which reaction is the inspired and prophetic one."*

*We are living in a period of transition. Our art is unconsciously groping
for a style which will best express the rhythm of our age.*

I cannot recall just when I first became aware that every great period of art seems to fit into one of two major styles — stylistic tendencies — of linear design. It was very probably in Paris in 1923, when I first began to collect children's drawings. At that moment children's drawings were very much in vogue. Scholarly and handsomely illustrated monographs were published about them in foreign editions. The work of five-year-olds was exhibited in Vienna, Paris and New York. I, too, fell under the spell of their innocent and ignorant charm. I was aware, as were many others, of the striking affinity between children's art and much of the best work of the Modern painters — Matisse, Chagall and the whole Cubist movement. I noted, however, that the fragile and unpredictable beauty of children's art is largely owing to the fact that a very young child has not the destructive intelligence and skill — acquired through years of patient effort at academic art schools — to duplicate a photograph or a chromolithograph with pencil, colored crayon or water color.

Upon one occasion I commissioned Léonine, a little French friend of eight years, to do a portrait of me for the modest sum of fifty centimes. Having stated the relation of body and head by two elliptical lines, she was confronted by the problem of attaching the arms, which do not grow from the neck but hang from the shoulders. By what graphic symbol could she properly solve this dilemma? Curiously enough it was by a convention which we find in all Javanese and to a lesser degree in Egyptian art, the creation of a false pair of shoulders from which the arms might hang. Elsewhere in the drawing were admirable graphic conventions for her observation of nature. She indicated the nose as a long cigar-shaped figure. But there are nostrils, and so the cigar was terminated by two tiny hooks — not a reproduction, but a free and personal symbol of a visual notation. The fingers were again indicated by long cigar shapes. Léonine was not impressed by the fact that hands have bones and knuckles; but she noticed that fingers have nails.

When the portrait was finished she decorated the margin of the paper with a simple formal pattern. "And now what color shall I paint you?" she asked.

"That, it seems to me, is a matter which, like the border, should be left to your taste and discretion."

Her eyebrows concentrated upon me for a moment. "I think I ought to paint you blue." she said.

Color to the adult artist as to the child is a far more personal and emotional expression than line. It is essentially felt. At any rate it does not contain within itself to the same degree as does the encircling line a noted fact of life. It communicates not so much a factual observation as a sensation. And thus it becomes part of a formal design, a rhythmic melody.

The decorative pattern encircling Léonine's portrait was an example of the child's inborn impulse to fit life and experience into some sort of a formal design. But why was it, I began to inquire, that the child should express this strongly felt, ingrained aptitude for formal design almost universally through the same linear elements that also characterize the great primitive schools — African, American Indian, Polynesian — and today Modern Art?

Studying these elements of graphic design, first in Japanese prints and later in children's drawings, it slowly dawned on me that they seemed generally to fall into two major, alternating, ever recurrent styles of design, appearing from the earliest times and in every nation: among primitive tribes and in the most sophisticated cultures, among trained artists, children or even the insane. And still later it became evident that each of these two stylistic approaches accompanied to a greater or lesser degree a different imaginative approach in the entire fabric of the civilization; a different attitude toward life, toward religion, and the solution of human problems.

Here I am treading new paths — or at any rate along paths which have not been clearly laid out. My effort will be to sketch in broad outlines a conception that can be immediately and easily understood. If I use specific examples it is to illustrate a general principle, not to dogmatize in detail. I shall be satisfied if I can establish a pattern of ideas that will give a better understanding of Modern Art in all its implications; with its failures and shortcomings as well as with its potential greatness. I feel that all of us should have the fullest understanding of the new language in which we are trying to speak — of its unique qualities and range as well as of its limitations. Perhaps what I suggest will help others to an even truer knowledge of the relation of formal design to the activities of the human mind and to our basic attitude and approach to life itself.

For the moment and for want of a better word I shall call the first of

these schools — or, more properly speaking, general tendencies of stylization — the Classical (including the neoclassical, the baroque, and so on)
Style of Design. With certain exceptions, we find it occurring in most
Western European art after fifth-century Greek art, through the Roman
and up to the Modern Movement of today. The exceptions are the art
of those periods that came under the influence of Islamic and Byzantine
civilization; also the Romanesque and Gothic, which were greatly influenced by and perhaps even had their origin in Byzantine art. It would be
wrong, however, to think of the Classical style, or stylistic tendency, as
solely a European or Western expression. At certain periods it crops up in
the earliest Egyptian, Indian and Chinese art, sometimes in the folk art
of Europe and the Far East, even in the art of Oceania and Alaska. In a
very general sense, however, it is that school of design which we associate with late Greek, Pompeian, Renaissance, baroque and recent European period styles up to the present.

Its characteristics are: the prevalence of the reverse curve or "line of
beauty"; the basic reliance on plant form and such motifs as we find in
leaves, buds, flowers; the tendency toward variation rather than repetition of the primary elements of design; the parsimonious reliance on the
use of such elements as the dot, dash, angle and straight line, and more
especially in a distaste of the repetition and the parallelism of such elements. The pictorial art of such periods is characterized by realism in the
representation of nature. (See Figs. 10, 12, 13, 19.) There is an avoidance
of symbolism and abstractions. There is a central unity of composition in
pictorial art and to a great degree in formal design.

The Corinthian column in Greek architecture, inspired by the acan-
thus leaf, and the use of the grape leaf in Renaissance design are typical
of the tendencies and antipathies of this general style. In either example
we have an ornate, somewhat intricate, easily recognizable type of design.
It is closely modeled on plant form. The pattern is constructed of segments of circles and segments of ellipses, flowing freely in never-ending
convolutions and variations of the reverse curve. (See diagram on p. 80.)

It is true that straight lines are sometimes introduced into such design.
They are never, however, used as a principal element of the leitmotif,
but rather — as often in the baroque and in the noblest of the Japanese
prints by Sharaku, Utamaro, Hokusai, Shunsho or Kiyonaga — as a bal-

ance wheel, storm anchor or antidote to the cloying effect of the ever-turning convolutions of the curve. So, many years ago among the Society Islands, I could let myself flow unrestrained into the winding, twisting, chaotic dance of the long-stemmed, feather-crested palms of the Pacific atolls, firmly supported, as they were, by the strength and weight of the

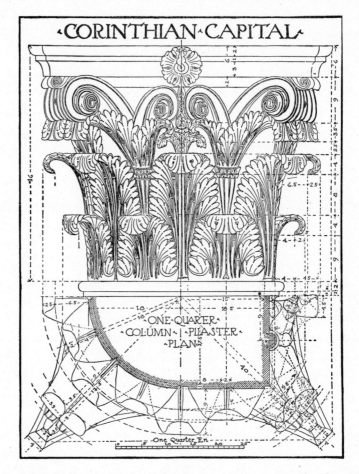

From Frank C. Brown, *Study of the Orders* (Chicago, 1906), Plate XVII

dark-blue horizontal sea. So today from my bedroom window, I can follow and participate in the dolfin-like upward and downward curving thrust of the branches of the ancient tulip poplar, shooting outward from a trunk that rises skyward, clean and straight as a ship's mast.

Yet with all its convolutions the Classical school must not be thought of as chaotic, indecisive, or meandering in style. Greek, Pompeian, Renaissance, baroque and the great periods of French art owe their achievement to the rigid, almost mathematical, control of the generously flowing curves. An over-all unity gives distinction and strength to the infinite variations of the dominant motif. We can describe it best as a style of sophistication, awareness and controlled exuberance. Without this control and perception, it could easily degenerate, as indeed in its debased forms it does, into the turgid and redundant tracery engraved on a calf's brain.

To summarize: the frequent reliance on plant form and the reverse curve, unity, symmetry, variation, an antipathy to repetition and parallel relations, and realism rather than symbolism or abstraction in the representation of nature, are the dominant characteristics of what I here speak of as the Classical Style of Design.

In Western pictorial art this style is seen perhaps at its noblest and most extreme in the baroque paintings of Michelangelo's "Last Judgment" and El Greco's "Burial of Count Orgaz" in the Church of Saint Thomas in Toledo. The composition of the "Last Judgment" is an incredible tour de force. For in the huge mural there is not even the indication of a straight line. And although the grouping of the individual figures is organized in the most masterly fashion, yet in final analysis what holds the whole mass together and prevents its collapse is not the internal design but the sheer compelling power and magnetic grip of the artist's vision.

To me El Greco's is the finer composition of the two (see Fig. 18). There is here an orchestration of music as rich and complicated as the larger motifs are simple and strongly felt. Although the various elements of the design caper, dance, twist, rise and circle like tongues of flame leaping toward the sky, yet the circular motif of the three central figures is framed and held together by the uprights of the figures to either side. The whole painting, in religious theme as in abstract pattern, is boldly cut in two, dividing earth from heaven. The horizontal line of faces and the downward counterthrust of the two supporting figures have the weight of an oak beam, of death and of life's despairing sorrow.

For it is true that dramatic incident and spiritual content can exert a counterthrust, give unity and a feeling of basic support to restless, tortuous and interpenetrating design. In the estimation of the Buddhist art of India, China and Japan, however, we are ignorant of the significance of the obscure religious symbolism and must depend in our appreciation on the enjoyment of the design and associative form. I sometimes experience a slight physical nausea before the writhing shapes, the swaying heads and serpentine limbs of oriental art. The twisting, wriggling calligraphy of some of the Chinese dragons of the Sung dynasty stirs in me only a feeling of impatience, frustration and apathy: impatience with the childish bombast and frustration with a line that neither contains form, nor has a beginning or an end. But the most debased oriental or Chinese calligraphy is never as bad, I am afraid, as some of the current styles of the macaroni-spaghetti marbleizing schools of contemporary art. For here one senses a complete disintegration of the esthetic tissues: not the heightened, oversensitive and chaotic awareness of the lunatic, but the soft, slow, spongy dribble of the cretin; the complete paresis of those human even more in pictorial art.

For the moment and for want of a better word, I shall designate the other major tendency in formal design as the Primitive Style of Design. But this designation has no necessary reference to primitive or immature expressions in art. I use it because of its general association with certain cultures. In Europe we find it in early Hellenic and Mediterranean art, usually prior to the fifth century B.C.; in Byzantine, Islamic and Gothic art (see Fig. 20). It is seen in the formal design of our Pueblo Indians and elsewhere among the Indians of Mexico, Peru and Chile (Figs. 16, 17). We find it in Africa, Polynesia and Australia. It occurs frequently in the drawings of lunatics, and of children up to adolescence (see Figs. 6, 7). Its elements form also the basic structural components — not of all Modern Art, but — of Modern Design.

We can already guess what these elements are, the relations into which they are brought together, and the other characteristics of this stylistic approach in design. A sympathy with geometric forms and the frequent use of the dot, dash, angle and straight line; the repetition through alternation or in parallel formation of these elements; an antipathy to the reverse curve and to the use of plant forms in formal design, and an an-

tipathy toward realism in representational art; the preference for stylization, symbolization and abstraction; the frequent neglect of central unity
of design and the occasional use of asymmetry both in formal design and
even more in pictorial art.

Americans will immediately recognize this style — or tendency in design — in all its purity and perfection in the pottery and paintings of the
Pueblo Indians. And having in mind, as the opposite pole, the Corinthian column of the Greeks or the convolutions of Renaissance orna-
mentation, the least scholarly person will recall the same elements and
relations of linear design in African sculpture, in the decorations of Greek
vases of the sixth century B.C., in the early Cubist paintings (see Fig.
8), the designs of modern fabrics (see Fig. 30), the geometric patterns
of Gothic or Romanesque stained-glass windows — in the simple angular
geometric patterns in the drawings of young children (see Fig. 6) and
the highly complicated geometric designs of Bokhara rugs and other Islamic decorations.

Futurism and the early phases of Cubism are a clear example of this
school of design in its purist form. They have all the characteristics of
which I have spoken: asymmetry; parallelism of elements; emphasis on
angles, straight lines, dots and dashes; antipathy to central unity of composition and the reverse curve; and most notably, of course, a distaste for
realism in its presentation of subject matter or nature. I do not want to
intimate, however, that one never finds the characteristic elements of
Classic Design in Modern Art. On the contrary, I would rather suggest
that, as in any great art expression — contemporary music or achitecture,
for example — there is an untrammeled freedom in the eager search for
and assimilation of elements from different and often incongruous styles.
And it is this combination of conflicting, inharmonious, inappropriate
and even discordant notes that gives that particular bitter and characteristic savor to the best of our contemporary art and music.

I can readily admit, too, that much of the painting of the Modern
Movement — of Matisse, Chagall, Dérain, Picasso and others — although
it is quite revolutionary in character and design, nevertheless does not
entirely depend on the use and the relations of those elements that I have
designated as "primitive." And other artists, notably affiliated with the
Modern Movement, have consciously modeled their design and composi-

tions on the baroque, on Rubens and El Greco; as even on early Renaissance art.

And what, one immediately asks, are the different approaches to life —
the prejudices, inclinations, apprehensions, assurances, religions, philosophies and basic assumptions — which generally seem to distinguish these
two "outward visual expressions" of the civilizations of the world?

For thirty years I have been groping for a satisfactory answer to this
question. It would seem to explain much not only of contemporary art
but of contemporary life. I could never feel that Modernism is merely a
capricious experimentation with line, color and design. Others — Goethe,
Spengler, Venturi and Toynbee — have noted the close relation between
any civilization and its particular expression in line, color or musical interval.

Four or five years ago I found myself walking with Amédée Ozenfant
along the old colonial logging road leading from the Finney Farm at Croton up to the high projecting ridge from which the noble view extends
northward to Bear Mountain Bridge and south to the Palisades and Spuyten Duyvil. We had come to lay at rest in a small clearing on top of the
ridge the remains of a dear friend. Returning through the upland pastures, now covered with second growth, we talked of people whom we
had known in Paris in the twenties, and of Ozenfant's recent book which
I had been reading. We speculated about the universal causes which
must have given birth to Modern Art. Ozenfant, who was himself among
its earliest exponents, fears, as I do, that its basic meaning and purpose,
never too clearly understood, is in danger of being smothered under the
high-pressured and frothy expressionism and the arid theorizing of an art
without either bones, sinews, or blood.

I told him how much I had been interested in his attempted explanation of the significance in art of the recurrent use of straight or curved
lines; * of how close his speculation was to mine; and how I believed that

* "Curves, language of sweetness, charm, grace, femininity. To draw, paint, sculpt,
practice architecture, dance, is so to dispose straight or curved forms and colors as to
provoke sensations and associations specific to each of them (so, too, with sounds in
music) . . .
   "When a particular kind of feeling is dominant in certain epochs, the general distribution of certain 'modes' creates what is known later as its 'style.' Modes depend on
manners of thinking and feeling, and not on technique: fashions of building, painting,

art and civilization itself could perhaps be expressed through linear design in terms of an extroverted or introverted approach to life. I felt that this extroverted or introverted approach would find its counterpart in what I have hitherto called the Classical and the Primitive styles in design.

---

writing, are determined by modes of feeling and thinking . . . In the fifth century the Greeks simultaneously constructed proud Doric temples and gentle Ionic ones. Two mentalities co-existed: the Doric severity at times yearned to soften in volutes. They were heroes by day, but at night in the camps they had their gentle captives" (Amédée Ozenfant, in *Foundations of Modern Art*).

MODERNISM: AN
INTROVERTED APPROACH

From the Author's Diary, December 10, 1947. I saw a good deal of Leo Stein in Paris in 1926. I remember his once saying to me, as he sipped his warm milk at the Café du Dôme: "Picasso was a talented draftsman, a dessinateur *in the grand French tradition of Ingres, Degas and Toulouse-Lautrec. His real tragedy is that he formed his style in a period when drawing, portraiture and illustration were in singular disrepute and decadence. It is this which probably accounts for his early and extreme preoccupation with Cubism and the abstract." Stein was as prejudiced as the next man in his esthetic judgments. But this is his personal opinion of a man whom he knew intimately, and therefore it carries some weight.*

May, 4, 1952. When will our art turn away from its present introverted or escapist abstractions and fantasies and grapple with life? Consider the twin poles of Byzantine and Renaissance art—the hierarchical, ideal, architectonic as opposed to the passionately observed, deeply felt, humanistic preoccupation with life. And yet at times the two poles have been fused, as in early Hellenistic art—Venus anodomine—in medieval sculpture and in the work of the great Japanese printmakers, Sharaku, Utamaro and Hokusai.

Among children drawing is never an esthetic outlet but primarily an idiom of speech, a method of communicating to a fellow being an observed fact of life. It is true that the child can communicate this new experience or observation in words, but words are symbols one step further removed from what he has visually experienced. The linear symbol will seem to the child a closer approximation to reality than the more indirect approach of the mind. I use the expression linear *symbol* rather than *representation* or *reproduction*.

The youngest child, as the most sophisticated artist, seems to sense that in this graphic language—as in any other—he can communicate an idea only through a sign, having a meaning. His symbols will fall into certain easily recognized patterns. Sometimes they will vary with the child's subconscious, intuitive approach. Thus at the daybreak of life there is created in its truest meaning style. For style is the crystallized idiom in a given medium best suited to communicate an imaginative idea.*.

From earliest years until maturity the growing child, in his slow, unconscious effort to readjust its ego to the impersonal detachment of the world's reality, swings from periods of extroversion, when he is curious, eager, absorbed with every new and exciting manifestation of the universe, to other periods of introversion, flights from reality, escape into the security of his own inner dreams and life. For in this deep and mysterious seclusion, he encounters no unfriendly and unyielding obstacle or barrier, but can re-create his own delicious universe, often merely of shapes, sounds and feelings and having little connection with an obdurate, static and already completed world.

In his stylized, abstracted, visual language the growing child gives expression to these two alternating, recurrent phases of human growth: the hasty withdrawing into his self-sufficient, brooding inner life and the tentative reaching-forth — fresh, eager, and madly excited. And it is this artless but highly emotional and deeply felt approach which lends such tender charm to this first extroverted phase of children's drawings. For apart from the innate and of course tentative and clumsy sense of rhythm or design — which, it is my unshaken belief, pulses through all human beings — a child is completely without any genuinely esthetic feeling, sense of beauty, or other mature reflection. But eagerness, ingenuousness, sensitivity and ruthless honesty — all childish qualities — are in themselves a source of joy. No wonder that Henri Matisse, who, though gifted in many ways, was perhaps lacking in both innocence and the child's excited wonder in the external world, could observe, on being shown the drawings of fourteen-year-old Pamela Bianca: "After seeing these, what is there left for me to do?"

In a somewhat later development, the child, having made his first visual contacts, swings back into a subconscious absorption with himself. Often in his drawings he creates whole series of symbols which may have

* Throughout this book I use "style" in the accepted broad dictionary definition of a "distinctive mode of presentation in any art."

deep significance to him, but which do not convey the intended meaning to someone else. The charming story was once told me of a city mother who was asked by her small offspring to admire what seemed to be range upon range of superimposed hills.

"But what are they; mountains?" the mother asked, "and wherever did you see them?"

The child's knitted brow evidenced her perplexity. "But do they have to be anything?" she retorted.

Peggy Bacon once told me that her eight-year-old daughter Belinda had been showing her the bewildering mazes and patterns of her younger brother Sandy. "Sandy is only interested in abstract art, mother," she explained with a note of finality. But I rather suspect that the less sophisticated Sandy, ignorant at once of Freud and of Modern Art, was quite content with the significance of his own self-expressive symbols. This second ingrown phase I often think of as the child's Expressionist or Non-objective manner.

From the point of view of child education, the importance of art is enormous, whether the medium be clay, carpentry, drawing, or the emotional use of color. It is the sanest and healthiest way to free the child from his emotional tangles and, by stimulating the creative process, to help him adjust to an external world. His actual production is often an illuminating graph of his particular problem. I once knew a child who only drew ladies with lorgnettes. Sometimes these were replaced by pince-nez or opera glasses. In one drawing of concentrated, subconscious tension, a dowager was drawn with spectacles; opera glasses were slung from her shoulder and she held a pair of eyeglasses in either hand. How Freud would have licked his chops over such an exposure!

Thus the child in his normal development swings from an absorption in and readjustment to the outer world to an introverted preoccupation with his own ego. Adolescence, when the curtain for the first time is lifted from the all-absorbing mystery of sex, is perhaps the last such inward-gazing period before emergence into the comparative maturity of manhood or womanhood. The adolescent steps forth from these incessant conflicts of growth, a near adult, with a compulsive drive to conform to the social adult pattern. No wonder that at this moment in our West

European or American culture the normal creative art impulse in ninety-nine out of a hundred is destroyed.

During these formative years the child has lived through recurrent cycles of creative expression. It seems clear that his inward-looking or introverted attitude toward life expresses itself through highly abstracted or geometric forms. On the other hand in his outward-looking, extroverted approach he tries to communicate his visual observations with representational symbols.

In considering the impulses which direct the growth and emergence of the artistic styles of different civilizations, let us hold in mind the analogy of these emotional directions and their stylistic expressions in a child's growth. They may help us to explain many phases of contemporary art which otherwise might be impossible to understand.

In contemporary life can we also point to an escape from reality, which will explain the striking similarity between those elements of design which characterize Modern Art and which are also present in the drawings of children and insane persons?

Children and primitive peoples evince their animistic approach toward the fury or beneficence of natural forces, which obviously they cannot control, and which they hope to propitiate. They endow these supernatural forces, ruthless or benign, with personalities that are capable of kindly gestures or ferocious appetites. There will be many shrewd and sensible ways with which to deal with and placate these divinities: good manners in their presence, the gratification of their whims, bribery, cajolery, and now and again a human sacrifice. But, as the average child knows too well, it rarely pays to reason with one's parents. And Reason and Science never influenced the approach of primitive people to the deities.

With few exceptions despotism has been the universal form of government from ancient times the world over. The dictator, buttressed by absolute power, is surrounded by a priestly class, which controls and censors for its own obvious advantage the fields of religion, education, science and politics. The common people, subjugated, wretched and superstitious, are held frozen in a state of perpetual dependence. In its most typical form this is the Oriental State, as it has always existed, as it exists today;

wherever, in fact, the life of reason and the belief in the dignity of the individual has not broken through the encircling net of ignorance, superstition and fear.

One can speculate whether the deeper need for religious faith, the prevalence of mysticism, and the greater emphasis on spiritual life which we associate with Oriental civilization is a logical result of the physical misery of the majority of human beings living under these conditions. We know, however, that all the great religions of mankind had their origin in the Orient or the Near East, under exactly such conditions of universal misery; and further that early Western Christianity and the medieval Age of Faith were born and flourished in Europe during those periods when black hopelessness and physical distress prevailed.

Here and there the world over there must have been moments — flashes of lightning in the darkness — when reason tried to break through the heavy fog of universal superstition, intolerance and prejudice. Greek civilization — through some mysterious chemical precipitation beyond historical analysis — was the first great and successful effort to assert its faith in reason and man's dignity, in its successful struggle with the prevailing oriental superstition and despotism, over the spirit as over the body of mankind.* Hellenic culture flashed up and flowered for a brief moment. Its influence — at least over Western thought — never thereafter completely died. So powerful was the original faith — the belief in reason, science, and man — that its tradition, ebbing and flowing through the centuries, has become and still is that of Western civilization. Today it is still in head-on conflict with the same oriental superstition and despotism, against which it was struggling twenty-five hundred years ago.

It would seem to follow as a matter of common sense that the Greeks, with their humanistic and scientific curiosity and their preoccupation with nature, should have made use of a realistic expression in their art.

---

* "The bias toward the rational that was to distinguish the West, and the deep spiritual inheritance of the East, were united. The full effect of this meeting, the immense stimulus to creative activity given when clarity of mind is added to spiritual power, can best be realized by considering what had happened before Greece, what happens, that is, when there is a great spiritual force with the mind held in obeyance . . . Greek art, Western art, is the unification of what is without and what is within. The complete mystic, expressionist, would never even desire to put into any concrete form the beatific vision . . .

"The studio of the Greek was not a lonely cave of meditation, but the world of moving life" (Edith Hamilton, in The Greek Way to Western Civilization).

And whenever else in the history of art — as in Chinese landscape painting of the Sung Dynasty and in Egyptian portraiture of the Old Kingdom — we find a realistic expression in art, we may safely presume a similar curiosity and preoccupation with the wonders of nature and the rational, outgoing, humanistic and unprejudiced mind.

If realism in art is characteristic of our Hellenic-West European tradition — the extroverted tradition of reason and humanism — what type
of design and pictorial art might logically reflect those introverted civilizations which place a greater emphasis on the things of the spirit than on
the things of the visual world? Among most primitive people, whose economic and political life was ritualistically enmeshed with their spiritual
beliefs, art is characterized by a highly abstract and symbolized expression.* Occasionally among highly civilized nations the same relation between a dominant religious faith and a highly abstracted art exists; † notably in Islamic, Byzantine and medieval Gothic art. Lastly, as has been
observed, the art of children and of lunatics is often symbolic and usually
highly abstract; and the cultural expression of neither children nor the
insane, absorbingly interesting though it is, fits into the pattern of the
rational and the humanistic approach to life.

Today the world sits on the edge of a volcano. Every taxicab driver
knows as much. For most thoughtful people life in their waking hours
has the logic and the lucidity of a nightmare. But long before World War
II and the Korean War, cracks could be seen in the picture, which up to
1914 had looked so rosy and seemed so solid. Confronted with the spectacle of the uses to which science could be marshaled in the creation of
the totalitarian state and the "realities of a social order so alien to human
personality and to human freedom, men and women in this century have,
not surprisingly, lost their sense of the old certainties. Science is known

---

* "The mystical artist always sees patterns. The symbol, never quite real, tends to
be expressed less and less realistically, and as the reality becomes abstracted the pattern
comes forward.

"Human figures . . . are made into patterns, schemated designs of the human body,
an abstraction of humanity. In the case of an Eastern rug all desire to express any sem-
blance of reality is gone. Such a work of art is pure decoration. It is the expression of
the artist's final withdrawal from the visible world, essentially his denial of the intellect"
(Hamilton, *The Greek Way to Western Civilizaztion*).

† "Indian art derives its basic character from certain ideals associated with the religious and philosophic outlook of India" (Jawaharlal Nehru, in *The Discovery of India*).

both as liberator and destroyer . . ." Yes, our optimism in the omnipo-
tence of science has been sadly shaken. "The core of contemporary disillusion," writes Barbara Ward, "is the conspiracy of industrialism, na-
tionalism, science, and mass communication to produce an inhuman order
of society." There has been, then, since the turn of the century and increasingly since the two World Wars, a disillusion with the unshaken
belief of the nineteenth-century that science will cure the ills of the
world. And it is not surprising after these irrational and futile holocausts
that there has been all through Western Europe a recrudescence of religious movements.

Aldous Huxley in a letter to me in 1940, in answer to a letter of mine
in which I had hoped to interest him in the urgency of Federal Union,
of which I was one of the National Directors, evinced his skepticism of
effecting any permanent cure for the ills of the world through even the
wisest and best-intentioned political channels. We should rather show
our concern, he felt, with those "kinds of philosophy and religion that
are antidotes to politics, namely mystical philosophy and a theocentric,
not anthropocentric or humanistic religion. . . You mention Jefferson,
whom I greatly admire. But if the Jeffersonian philosophy is to be ap-
plied, it is surely clear that the human lump must be leavened by an ap-
preciable number of people whose concern is with mystical philosophy
and theocentric religion . . . Woolman might have imitated his neighbor, Franklin, and gone into public life. By remaining marginal and
keeping alive the spirit of American Quakerism, he probably has been of
more benefit to his country than Franklin has been . . ."

Right or wrong I quote this passage as a fair example of the shift
among many of our intellectuals from a material and humanistic philosophy to a more mystical and religious approach. Bertrand Russell on
his eightieth birthday, in reviewing a life devoted to a faith in rationalist
philosophy, at the core of which he had placed the study of mathematics,
could say: "What the world needs is more charity, more Christian compassion, more love."

American artists, too, are groping to express in their work something
more eternal than the laws of light and color, which so intrigued the
early Impressionists, or even the face of Mother Nature to which the

Master of Aix payed homage. Yasuo Kuniyoshi commented on his own development in a letter to Ralph Pearson: "During this period (1929–1938) I was attracted to the visual object because of its shape, color, design or even associative quality. That was *one* of the motivating factors in painting it, but gradually the inner meaning became more important and the thoughts it evoked became my main object in painting."

And Peppino Mangravite says of himself: "And now I seem to be deeply preoccupied with the Universe within man."

And Rico Lebrun: "My true task here is that the forms themselves should carry meaning of terror and pity . . . I want more connotations of universality."

And Samuel Adler: "What we are looking for is cosmic order. It is elusive. But when one gains order one knows peace . . . I paint, not what I see, but what I feel; not what I think, but rather what I am, since art, as I reason it, is the articulation of man's intellectual, spiritual, and esthetic impulses in relation to life as experience." *

Such convictions evidence the growing disillusion of thoughtful men, artists and scientists with the hard, clear, self-assured positivism of nineteenth century philosophy. In an attempt to estimate the force and direction of certain contemporary trends, I shall indicate to what degree this religious or mystical preoccupation seems to be one of the motivations of American art. At present I am considering the possible relation of certain styles of design and the approach toward life of those civilizations and periods in which they occur.

But we can say with assurance that most Modern artists are passionately convinced that the Modern Idiom best expresses the world of today: the world which was born between the turn of the century and the First World War, at that moment in history which marked the end of the five-hundred-year cycle introduced by humanism, science and the Reformation.

The final and mature artistic expression of Modernism is not yet clearly stated, for our New World is still in the throes of evolution. What will it be? A shout of confidence? The tired smile of disillusion? A whimper of despair? Today it is a little of all three.

* The quotations above are from Ralph M. Pearson, *The Modern Renaissance in American Art* (New York: Harpers, 1954).

I had best immediately, however, state the terms on which I believe that answer depends. It would seem true that nations and civilizations, after the pattern of the growth of children, in the process of their development and decay continually gravitate between the preoccupation with the outer world and a belief in its control through science and intelligence, and an inner preoccupation with the things of the spirit. The complete and extreme surrender to either point of view will invariably result in a lopsided and barren culture: the shallow materialism of nineteenth-century capitalism or the fatalism and physical degradation of oriental despotism. The mature human being, or nation, or art expression, will always show the appropriate balance between mind and spirit, science and religion, the outward- and the inward-looking eye. Such was the art of Greece, of French medieval architecture, of Renaissance painting. Modern Design is the vessel which will contain the Modern Art of the Modern World. The form and pattern of the vessel is now clearly defined and shaped. Unless our artists can pour into it a human draught, its taste will be watery and thin.

13'

LIMITATIONS OF
THE ABSTRACT

*From the Author's Diary, January 16, 1948. Discussing the other
day with Arthur Malsin the limitations of nonobjective art, I readily admitted
that some people may derive their fullest esthetic pleasure and satisfaction
from abstract painting. Its limitation is, however, the general lack of communication. It can never hope for a universal or even a comparatively wide
appeal; for the same obvious reason that poetry, written in a language foreign
to the reader will not give as much satisfaction as it does to those who understand the words. Fundamentally it is a question of common sense.*

*"But how," asked Malsin, "do you account for the universal appeal of
music, which generally speaking cannot be identified with a concrete experience of life?"*

*This is a question which has puzzled many of us. The answer is, I think,
that although music, like all the arts, is an intuitive re-creation of life, yet it
is not identifiable with a material object. In that sense it is not a representational art form — any more than architecture or landscape gardening — in the
same sense that words or pictures identify the lived and seen realities of our
world. It is in the nature of color and line that their design stirs us most deeply
when integrated with an experience of life or a useful object. It is in the nature
of music that we enjoy it most in a highly abstract form, disassociated from a
representational world. Yet in the Spenglerian sense, as in John Dewey's
understanding of the meaning of art, music is as much the expression of a culture, the intimation of a human experience, as is Dante's Divine Comedy or
El Greco's "Burial of Count Orgaz."*

*February 6, 1951. I visited the exhibition of American abstract art at the
Museum of Modern Art. Of the six artists whose work seemed to me highly
personal and outstanding, five were born before 1881: Marin in 1870, Feininger in 1871, Stella and Hartley in 1877, Weber in 1881. Stamos alone is of
a younger vintage, born in 1922. The elder group painted their abstractions
between 1912 and 1918; Stamos, in 1948. The rest of the work in the exhibition seemed to me essentially in the nature of rather cold and intellectual-*

ized industrial design — sometimes good; more often fabricated, insensitive,
and without any inventive or creative spark. Moving suddenly from these
galleries, which contained so much academic and overpublicized rubbish, and
into the galleries of contemporary sculpture, where were assembled the works
of Lehmbruck, Maillol, Barlach, Marini, Lachaise, Epstein, Zorach and Nadel-
man, I felt as if my lungs were breathing fresh sea air after too long a visit in
a sick room — or a candy factory.

There is no doubt that much of the best art today — the most creative,
imaginative, and personal — is less preoccupied with nature, portraiture
and the externalized world than was the case up to the death of Cézanne.
Nor can there be any doubt as to the beauty and sensitivity of many abstract and nonobjective paintings. The other day in the National Gallery
in Washington, lingering before some of the early Cubist canvases of
Picasso and Braque, I felt again, as I had forty years ago when I first saw
them, the spontaneity, youth and exuberance with which those fresh
young eyes had looked out upon the bright colors and explosive designs
of their New World.

Art theories are at best trial balloons, and the roundest and tightest,
when pricked, may sink to the ground. Anything that succeeds is successful. A living abstract painting is preferable to a dead transcription of
the living world. For art deals essentially with life, and the latter cannot
be four-footed and pigeon-holed, hog-tied and Yale-locked by any number
of art theories on two or two thousand sides of the question. Since the
creative instinct is unpredictable and not an affair of logic, it may still
jump the analysis of *a priori* speculation. In retrospect, however, we can
look back — for it is a thing of the past — on the Paris school of 1900–
1920. It was a greatly stimulating, ground-plowing, introspective, psychoanalytic movement: critical of old values, proposing new cures, youthful,
ingrown, narrow, genial, essentially honest, and charged with creative
fertility. That highly sophisticated and metropolitan movement, turning
its back on the visual world, rationalized its definition of art as something
pure, abstract and within a vacuum.

Such, then, was the flavor of this new draught — Abstract Art —
which in the first decades of the century was poured into a newly-fash-
ioned vessel — Modern Design. The validity of abstract art is unquestioned. But what are its inherent limitations?

Again and again its protagonists have adduced the analogy of music in postulating the emotional range of nonobjective painting as a legitimate — in fact the most legitimate — idiom of pictorial expression. But in this assertion they are unconsciously guilty of a very grave omission and an equally grave error, both having to do with the misuse of medium. And the misuse of medium, as every sound craftsman knows, goes to the very root of creative utterance.

In music the abstract — that is, nonrepresentational — idiom can express ninety-nine per cent of all that music has to say. For the melody that tinkles like a bell, thunders like a storm, or bleats like a lamb, conveys all in all the emotional response of a penny whistle. On the other hand, the most fantastic theorist could never assert that the representational element in painting — in Rembrandt's portraits, Goya's "Horrors of War," Daumier's cartoons, or Turner's landscapes — has added nothing that cannot be equally well expressed by nonobjective art. In other words — beautiful and valid as it often is — abstract painting is consciously limiting the scope of its message to an infinitesimal fraction of what "this most beautiful of all media" can say. Now this omission can have consequences as dangerous as total atrophy of expression. Does this mean that artists should consciously avoid the abstract? No more, I should say, than Elizabethan poets avoided the occasional use of a "Hey, nonny, nonny." But those artists — or schools of art — who consciously avoid the representational idiom, although they may create works of beauty, are thinning their expressive medium to a point where "bright, deft and smart" though it be, it is in danger of giving birth to a child without "bowels, carnality, sexuality or stomach." *

So much, in their misuse of the medium, for the *omission* of the greatest reservoirs of expression. But I believe that abstract and nonobjective artists are often also guilty of an equally grave error in the *use of the medium of oil paint* at all. For abstract, nonrepresentational designs can almost always be rendered in other media — stained glass, ceramics,

* "[John Burroughs] was afraid that American literature might lose its connection with the viscera and the blood and become an expression merely of intellectual quickness, for, as he wrote to Edward Dowden, the Irish admirer of Whitman, the rising writers ran to 'mere refinement.' They seemed to him of the superficial sort, knowing, quick, bright, deft and smart, but without port, bowels, carnality, sexuality or stomach, unlike the first crop of American writers" (Van Wyck Brooks, in *The Times of Melville and Whitman*).

mosaics — in more glowing and refulgent colors and more permanent form. One cannot help wondering whether intellectual apathy or a sensuous unresponsiveness to surface texture — wood, glass, silk, enamel or the *al fresco* technique — inhibits the exploration of these richer and more durable elements. For oil paint on canvas is in many respects a most unhappy medium. Subject to decomposition through moisture, the darkening effect of binders, chemical adulteration, cracking, rotting, tearing or other process of decay, an oil painting often loses its original brilliance during the life of its creator. Few can survive without serious deterioration for a matter of centuries. Mosaics, ceramics and enamel ware, on the other hand, if preserved with moderate care, in as many thousands of years will not appreciably lose their natural brilliancy.

Yet for all its deficiencies — its mutability, impermanence and lack of luster — oil painting has one quality which more than compensates for its many imperfections, and which has raised it during the past five hundred years to its position of preëminence among the graphic media. It has more fluidity, elasticity and malleability, and therefore lends itself more readily to the precise control of line and delicate shade of color than any other known medium. And thus little by little over the years in the hands of artists, curious as to the fleeting indication of human character and intrigued by every transition and delicate nuance of the sky, oil painting reached its fullest, richest, most personal and varied expression. It is somewhat ironic that those particular aspects of visual experience which oil paint is most perfectly designed to convey — the translucency of flesh, the transparency of atmosphere, the qualities of surface textures and the delicate characterizations of human personalities — are particularly those subjects, the blood and bones of the externalized world, in which the nonobjective artist has lost all interest. To sum up the anomaly of abstract painting: it can almost always be more beautifully and permanently executed in other media, such as ceramics or mosaics; while oil paint, on the other hand, has an innate superiority for those very purposes which lie beyond the preoccupations and goal of the nonobjective artist.

I have myself worked for over thirty years in the various craft media which I have mentioned. My feeling for their distinctive relevance and splendor is not entirely theoretic. Any sensitive craftsman knows that a particular design or pictorial idea is most appropriately embodied in a given material. It is of course universally admitted that abstract Modern Design has found successful expression for more than a generation in all the crafts: in furniture, light fixtures, the beautiful glass and silverware of the Scandinavian countries, in printed materials, the streamlining of automobiles and airplanes; in sum, in the decoration of every known useful object. Yet our nonobjective artists are rarely concerned with the crafts. They seem under the hallucination that an abstract pattern, carried out in an inadequate and transitory medium and isolated from a living world in a gilded frame on a museum wall, obtains thereby a certain cachet or significance, which it would miss if it merely enhanced and were integrated with the form of a useful object.

The abstract artist may retort that the work of art which he has created does far more than this. The esthetic emotion which his painting conveys can be identified with a lived and human emotion. And thus, he will assert, it is an expression of life, as is the case with any other work of art. But this is only true if the abstract painting can communicate an idea, impart an identical emotional response to the degree, for instance, that a symphony of Beethoven, a fugue of Bach, or a modern ballet will communicate the same emotional response in the average sensitive audience. Is such the case? I doubt it.

Nothing that I have said adds up to a categoric indictment of abstract or nonobjective painting. For in art — not in logic — the proof is in the eating of the pudding. Abstract painting has certain inherent limitations. I have tried honestly to indicate them. The most stringent qualification, however, is something other than an actual defect. There are many abstract paintings with freshness, beauty, and intuitive magic. There are a few which move me. But they can never be classed with the greatest art, for they do not deal with the deepest human emotions — love, death, birth, piety, tenderness, or even carnality.* Nor for the same reason can they

* The same fear of dealing directly with basic human emotions is also noticeable in much current literature. "Writers in general have reached a sort of North Pole, an 'icy aloofness from humanity,' as Peter Viereck sees them; and, standing at absolute North as they do, whichever way they face, their next step can only be 'toward the broad southlands of humanity.' The great original writer of genius who will dominate the coming time is almost certainly destined to take this step . . .

"Although the literary rank and file always naturally take for granted the absoluteness and permanence of the modes of any given present, these modes are mutable, they ever aspire to a great human audience over a length of time. For the assumption that nonobjective painting allows the artist the fullest expression of his medium would seem to involve an obvious escape from reality and common sense. Is it not that "denial of the validity of the will and human dignity" of which Lionel Trilling speaks in his *Liberal Imagination?* The world is "out of joint," and he is perhaps right in asserting that "the greatest psychological fact of our time which we observe with baffled wonder and shame is that there is no possible way of responding to Belsen and Buchenwald . . . Surely the great work of our time is the restoration and reconstruction of the will."

Somerset Maugham believes that when the artist can no longer grapple with the drama — the Yes and No — of life, even the most gifted will turn inward and spend his genius on the "quick, bright, deft and smart" embellishment of his craft. In his chapter on El Greco in *Don Fernando* he suggests that the baroque was essentially a preoccupation with design by a period which had lost its primary interest in nature and lived realities. Whether he is on solid ground or not in this particular instance, his thesis fits in well with my own conclusions about the limitations of abstract art. He writes: "When you rob the artist of [his freedom, as was the case when it was destroyed by the intolerance of the counter-reformation of the Catholic Church in the sixteenth century] you force him back upon himself. When he can no longer deal with the great issues of life that in happier times occupy the souls of men, his instinct of creation, which nevertheless demands expression, can but turn to decoration . . . The Renaissance, essentially objective, copied and idealised nature, but baroque used nature as a vehicle to display its own morbid sensibility. It was subjective. And the most direct expression of the subjective is decoration . . . All artists . . . if they lack serious and great convictions are very likely to squander their faculties on spiritual kickshaws . . . And it may be that the interest in formal design of the present day is due to the same causes as produced baroque art in the sixteenth century. Now too we are at sixes and sevens. Afraid of the sublime, we take refuge in the multiplication table.

"Liberty throughout the world is dying or dead . . . Artists have not

---

are destined to change, while the constant need remains to rehumanize whatever is dehumanized in life or in art" (Van Wyck Brooks, in *The Writer in America*).

yet learnt how to deal with what really matters to our world and so are driven to devote themselves to decoration. They make technical devices the end and aim of their endeavour." *

For this escape from life is without any doubt the gravest pitfall that lies in front of the full and healthy growth — not of Modern Design, which is already a mature stylistic expression — but of Modern Art, the creative expression in that style. Nor is it the individual abstract work of art which is ever in question. For that stands squarely on its own feet above the plane of rationalization. But the critical philosophy, the credos and manifestos of those groups of artists who would narrow the scope of traditional art, who assert that representational art is an outmoded expression, who would have us believe that the nonobjective idiom can convey the highest, deepest and clearest expression of the New World, are a paralyzing influence on the artist and public alike. For this ever-narrowing, devitalizing, and blood-thinning stricture on the normal vitality, curiosity, exuberance and many-sided individuality of the artist, although it is a thing of the moment, can affect and retard a healthy creative development.

For those who feel — as many will — that my position is colored with prejudice, I would only rejoin that, standing before the individual work of art, one should remain dispassionate, eager only to understand and evaluate the significance of the individual artist's intuitive reaction to life. But in one's attitude toward a current esthetic philosophy, which is harmful to artist and public alike, I believe a little healthy prejudice is the order of the day.

I think of Pablo Picasso as an outstanding genius but as something of a charlatan and a dangerous influence on young artists. In this instance however, his example may serve. He has created some of the greatest abstract paintings. He has turned out an exceeding amount of nonobjective trash. He has constantly — as in some of his very beautiful recent lithographs — returned to the orthodox, representational, and story-telling mode of traditional art.

* W. Somerset Maugham, *Don Fernando, or Variations on Some Spanish Themes,* pp. 255–258. Copyright 1935 by W. Somerset Maugham; reprinted by permission of the author; of Doubleday and Company, New York; and of Messrs. William Heineman, Ltd., London.

14'

EXPRESSIONISM:
A DEAD END

From the Author's Diary, January 21, 1948. I took part this morning in a round-table discussion at the Museum of Modern Art, subsequently to be recorded and televised, on the fundamental distinctions and affinities between Modern and Traditional Art. I was asked more or less to defend the traditional form of art; and Ben Shahn, the modern. But as I had anticipated, our points of view were so nearly identical that the discussion will have to be presented along different lines.

I had not seen Ben, for whose paintings I have the deepest admiration, since 1936, when we were both in Washington, I working on my Justice Department mural. We had gone together to the C.I.O. Headquarters in the hope of establishing closer relations between left-wing, socially conscious labor, and left-wing, socially conscious artists. At the meeting we had encountered a wall of suspicion and silence. Neither of us perhaps then fully realized that intellectually and politically American labor is essentially conservative.

I remember him then as red-haired, vivid and handsome. Now he is physically a little ponderous, with heavy, immobile features. His manner is somewhat pontifical and didactic. But he has an excellent, clear mind; talks slowly with great honesty; and obviously has thought out carefully what he has to say. He made two or three points that interested me.

Speaking of Mondrian he said: "We must be charitable and remember that the importance of certain artists' works is that they can be considered as steps, often groping and experimental, toward an important achievement." Undoubtedly true, I felt; but many of such experiments of a technical nature had best be kept in the laboratory, where they belong, rather than exposed in museums as definitive works of art.

Speaking of Expressionism he said: "In the Renaissance an artist, commissioned to paint a mural, was obviously thinking of his audience. But the egocentric emphasis of Modernism has brought about a different approach. The artist often today thinks only of pleasing himself and so, even though a mural painting concerning a matter of general interest may call for its clear interpretation by the general public, there is a total lack of communication between painter and audience." This, I said to myself, is obviously true of the "Guernica Mural" — one of Picasso's most important paintings and most successful efforts in semi-abstract Modern Design. The various symbols, which to Picasso denoted fascism, hatred, cruelty, and so on, will not be similarly identified by others.

It was the tragedy of André Gide, as with so many other frustrated intellectuals of his generation, that in his later years he oscillated between his defeatist disillusion with liberal humanism and his artist's faith in the importance in his own message.* Hopeless as seemed to him at times the survival of democratic freedom, he could still beautifully speak of Christianity as "cette incomparable école d'individualisation, où chacun est plus precieux que tous." And could he better have thus summed up the importance of the individual's expression in art, unfettered by political dogma, bureaucratic censorship or the suffocating weight of majority opinion?

Actually, of course, this emphasis on the individual's expression in art was the early fruit of the Italian Renaissance, ripened by the French romantic movement of the nineteenth century, and more recently still by the influence of psychoanalysis. Up to that time, however, Expressionism had created nothing more extreme than Rimbaud's poetry, Wagner's music or the paintings of Van Gogh; for Expressionism still flowed through the deeply worn channel of traditional art.

Modern Art, seen in retrospect, was essentially a preoccupation with form; and inevitably this preoccupation led in Modern Design to the abstraction of realism and to nonobjective art. But there was another element, besides this interest in pure form and design, which was responsible for the development of abstract painting: Expressionism — the right of the artist to paint nature, not the way it actually looked, but the way he felt like painting it.

Once again it is the story of my portrait by nine-year-old Léonine, who, after having considered me with soul-searching concentration, had concluded: "I think I will paint you blue." Is this a preoccupation with

* "11 septembre, 1939. Ma pensée retourne à son interrogation: Est-ce-là le crépuscule du soir, ou l'aurore?" (André Gide, in *Pages de Journal*).

design or the expression of Léonine's ego? Or the charming incident which René d'Harnoncourt once told me of a little Mexican Indian artist, who was selling his paintings to American tourists. In one of his pictures he had painted a brightly feathered and valiant rooster standing on the roof of a small house and crowing most lustily to all his world.

"But why, little man, have you painted the cock bigger than the house?" he was asked by a literal-minded lady client. Obviously he had never felt it necessary to consider this problem. He gazed at her through his darkly lashed, brooding Indian eyes before answering: "But, lady, this is *not* a cock and this is *not* a house. It is the *picture* of a cock and the *picture* of a house." Design or Expressionism? Again hard to say.

Expressionism had been an influence in European art long before Modernism. The subjective approach characterized the work of such artists as Jean Jacques Rousseau, Byron, Baudelaire, Wagner, Gauguin and Van Gogh. In the abstract idiom of Modern Art it found the mode par excellence into which to channel its subjectivity. But its use of the abstract idiom was quite other than that of the Cubist painters. The one school was intent upon the study of design, the other was seeking a channel of self-assertion. In each case there is a shift of emphasis from subject matter to the mode in which the subject is presented. But in the one case the emphasis is on the artist's formal style of treatment, in the other, on the subjective content of the artist. It could be said that the Cubists proclaimed the self-sufficiency, in art, of form. The Expressionists voiced the self-sufficiency of the artist.

I recall a visit to my Paris studio from Leo Stein during the winter of 1923. In his categoric and convoluted style he was explaining to me what he considered Matisse's most important contribution in the field of art, something which made him unique in the history of Western painting. "Hitherto," said Leo, "the artist has looked at his model, and concentrating his attention on that particular feature, color tone or inner quality which most appeals to his artistic sensibility, he has tried to let the expression of that unique attribute flow subconsciously onto the canvas through his intuitive line or brush-stroke. But Matisse's approach is quite different. He does not concentrate on any quality in his sitter, but on the *responsive emotion in himself,* which the sitter has evoked, and then on the intuitive expression on the canvas of *his own sensation.*"

I followed all this with a good deal of difficulty. It was many years later that I realized that Stein had very simply described to me the approach of any Expressionist painter.

When Benedetto Croce in 1902 proclaimed that art is nothing more than imaginative expression, he paved the way for the divorce of representational subject matter from Modern Art and lent emphasis to the importance of originality and individuality in the artist's intuitive expression of life. I do not mean that the young artists in Paris read Croce's *Estetica* or were in any way consciously influenced by him. Rather that his esthetics justified and gave coherence and meaning to their most radical experiments. In the field of criticism he elaborated a philosophic sanction on which their advocates could lean. For "expression" is the word more than any other that one associates with Croce's esthetics. It is the equation between the creator and the chaos of life, between the potter and his clay; which in Dewey's philosophy becomes "experience," and in my own thinking, a "reaction to life." Croce asserts: "Beauty is successful expression." "Ugliness is inexpressiveness." And further, that imaginative expression, since it has no intention, cannot will it. For expression is without purpose and so is incapable of employing techniques, which are always merely the means to an end. Expression can create a work of art — a painting, poem, or musical composition — only if it is also accompanied by an act of will.

Dewey, on the other hand, defines the creative act as the participation in any activity, so as to sublimate it into a human experience beyond its usefully intended purpose. I find this approach more sympathetic. As I try to analyze my own feelings as a creative artist, it seems impossible to split apart and to pigeon-hole the various elements — the inspiration, reaction, act of will; the physical and the material environment — all of which play their part in the eventual performance.

Paris just before the First World War was experiencing a period of feverish and speculative creative activity, eclectic and internationally minded, a little *fin de siècle*, with its roots never running very deep into the bowels of the times but sucking their sustenance from the smoke-filled atmosphere of Montmartre cafés. Quick, clever, genial, it had a jack-rabbit mentality, never quite following a straight line, and a little too eager, through a deftly executed *volte-face,* to leave the slower-footed public philistines baying up the wrong track.

Its preoccupation with theory, credos and ultimate dogma is, however, characteristic of the French genius, which has always searched in its art for precision of statement, rationality and formal exposition. Yet the movement was wholly lacking in French restraint, good taste and equipoise. It had, notwithstanding all this, created a style which has stamped itself upon the world. Our American temper and genius is born of a different tradition, and is most fertile when it springs from the belly rather than the head. Some would prefer to say from the heart rather than the mind. And it may be safely inferred that those American artists who continue to express themselves in the borrowed idiom of the Ecole de Paris, will continue to create a colonial art. For making this reservation I may be accused of chauvinism. But to me it is rather a matter of common sense. The accent and spoken style of a Down-Easter can always be distinguished from the idiom in use south of the Potomac.

Expressionism, however, is without any doubt one of the chief characteristics of Modern Art. In the hands of great or sensitive artists — of Van Gogh, Chagall, Marin, Klee, Weber, Rouault (Figs. 3, 5, 9, 32), James Joyce, Kafka or Stravinsky — it can be a powerfully moving factor. It is merely obnoxious when paraded by those who have nothing of importance to say. Among the Fauves it is always to me a little distasteful. And how much has it improved the color, design, mood and texture of the works of such other painters as Matisse, Munch, Dérain, Kokoschka or Soutine?

No matter how we assess the quality of Expressionism in the evaluation of a work of art, we shall agree that with all the artists I have named it is an element, conscious or unconscious, of distortion. This element of distortion, by its nature and to the degree with which it is exaggerated, is distasteful and perplexing to the layman, the uninitiate. Its esthetic intent, apart from any mere lack of technique or awkwardness, must be to emphasize and underscore the importance of the individual approach, which is so characteristic of our times. Georgia O'Keeffe tells of herself somewhere that in a moment of doubt in her own development she lined all her canvases against the wall. Looking at them one by one she set aside in the discard all of those which she felt did not express the essence of her personality. What was left could give her a line that thereafter she was to follow. This is a perfect example of the sincere artist, who is afraid not to be himself. One can, however, hardly imagine a cinquecento painter thus protecting the purity of his ego from contamination. These artists stole ravenously from one another and from the past; they were so hungry to absorb all there was to learn and had, too, such confidence in their own healthy assimilative powers of digestion.

Used with discretion the distortions of Expressionism can add tartness, sharp flavoring, the sliding out of true pitch into discord which is so relished by sensitive teen-aged music fans in our "blues." But even in these instances it is a little self-conscious and without that — equally expressive — dignity which flows from the line of a great artist — a Rembrandt, a Hokusai, a Degas. The unmistakable individuality of such painters is a harmonious confirmation of what they were intent on saying, while with lesser artists this continual emphasis on the personal approach has the effect of smothering in their own ego the little which they have to offer.

But more recently, and very much today, Expressionism has assumed a totally different role. It is no longer an emphasis, an attitude, an approach, which will more effectively slant the presentation of the work of art. It has become — just as nonobjective art has become — a mirror, a manifestation, an interpretation of the mood of the age in which we live. "The typical contemporary artistic productions," writes Enzo Paci, "clearly reflect the general uneasiness about the crisis of our values and our fear that the end of our civilization may be at hand . . . Franz Kafka provides a striking example . . . Or take Sartre. Fear, engendered by highly unstable social and political relationships and the recognition of the ambiguity of all situations, is the basic theme of his work . . .

"Form is torn apart in a violent analytical process that leads to the threshold of chaos such as in German Expressionism after the First World War . . . Expressionism is ruled by anarchical freedom, by the inarticulate cry [see Figs. 24, 25, 26]; abstractionism by stern, bare, nonhuman construction [see Figs. 22, 23]. The most recent abstract painting tries desperately for a world of new shapes, beyond the natural and human; it frequently succeeds in depicting the sub-human emanations of the sub-conscious that have not yet attained form or maturity. All these experiments in art point to the crisis of living, the gulf between freedom and harmonious order; consequently they express the failure to strike a balance between freedom and justice in social relations." *

To some of our museum directors, to the so-called avant-gardist crit-ics, and to art teachers in many of our schools and colleges, extreme and unlicensed Expressionism is in itself the flesh and blood of creative art. What fifty years ago was considered by Dewey and the psychoanalytic schools as a healthy therapeutic technique for educating children or re-solving their suppressed maladjustments to life has now become a valid form of painting and sculpture. It is worthwhile hearing what some of our contemporary artists say — recognized painters, teachers, writers and lecturers. Not that in any way a painting can be judged or condemned by the artist's rationalizations, but because to understand painting it is some-times helpful to understand what the painter is trying to express, and also the conditions in his environment that have made this approach pos-sible.

As sober and distinguished an artist as John Marin wrote about him-self: "It is this moving of me that I try to express, so that I may recall the spell I have been under and behold the expression of the different emo-tions that have been called into being. How am I to express what I feel so that its expression will bring me back under the spell?" †

Adolph Gottlieb writes: "I have always worked on the assumption that if something is valid or meaningful to me, it will also be valid and meaningful to others. Not to everyone, of course. On the basis of this assumption I do not think of an audience when I work, but only of my own reactions . . . If what I paint is expressive, if it seems to communi-cate the feeling that is important to me, then I am not concerned if my work does not have the well-known earmarks of art." ‡

And Esteban Vicente: "I could not explain what I had in mind or

* Enzo Paci, in *Contemporary Art as the Expression of the Social and Political Situ-ation.*

† Pearson, *The Modern Renaissance in American Art.*

‡ This and the following quotations are from *University of Illinois Exhibition of Contemporary American Painting, 1952* (Urbana: University of Illinois Press, 1952).

what I felt when I painted *Number 6* in particular. My paintings are a sequence of related sensations to which I attempt to give definite form. Each one represents an aspect of my total experience."

Hans Hofmann, a mature and sophisticated modernist, who has taught for over a generation in Europe and America, writes: "Every work of art represents a new Reality which exists nowhere else outside of its own existence. It is always a 'spiritual' reality, and as such it represents another — a new — pearl in the string of human documentation. A work of art is documented by a common denominator. This common denominator is the personality of the artist — his soul and his mind, his sensibility and his temperament. Through it 'experience' is summarized into pictorial language — that is to say, into a pictorial message." (See Fig. 25.)

This quotation is a fairly lucid statement of the doctrine of self-revelation. But the new spiritual reality, this pearl of human documentation, is not revealed by any transcendental Deity, but by Hans Hofmann to Hans Hofmann.

Knud Merrild, who has taught and published books and articles on Modern painting, describes his own "personal, intuitive expression" and the technical devices he uses in his painting: "Everything seems to depend on the whim or law of chance, accidental judgment by accidental authority and forced cause. And by chance and accident we live and die. To reflect this, I attempt a personal intuitive expression, where 'laws' of esthetic evaluation become meaningless. Therefore I do not subscribe to any former concepts . . .

"Flux painting consists of applying liquid colors to a fluid surface by pouring, dripping, or other means. A natural consequence of the process is that orthodox tools are of little use, being replaced by gravitation. The paint is expelled at various distances, from zero to several feet above the surface — painting by remote control. The pattern created differs according to the velocity or gravitational force, and to the density or fluidity of the paint. The impact of the expelled paint with the fluid surface creates fissions or explosive eruptions, more or less violent, and the painting is set in motion in four dimensions. Mutations follow, lasting from seconds to several hours. When in motion, incessant mutations of color and form ensue, until arrested in a metaphor of its own Flux. Left alone, it becomes an automatic creation by natural law, a kinetic painting of the abstract. It can be interfered with, intuitively, or controlled by a preconceived vision, as shown in my work."

How much confidence such a technique will inspire in those of us who may be more interested in the world about us than in the artist's "accidental" and "personal intuitive expression," is a moot point. There is no question, however, that this philosophy and these techniques are taken in all seriousness by far too many artists and critics alike. What is more frightening is that they should appeal to thousands of young art students, many of them talented, all through the nation.

The extreme Abstract Expressionist has divorced himself from nature and lived realities. He has consciously and willfully divorced himself from any possible communication with other human beings. He would also divorce himself, consciously and willfully, from the concern with any idea or any association with traditional art, or, almost it would seem, from any human emotion.

Adolph F. Reinhardt, who has also taught art and whose name is known on the museum circuit list, writes of himself: "Today many artists like myself refuse to be involved in some ideas. In painting, for me — no fooling-the-eye, no window-hole-in-the-wall, no illusions, no representations, no associations, no distortions, no paint-caricaturings, no dream pictures or drippings, no delirium trimmings . . . no mannerisms or techniques, no communications or information, no magic tools, no bag of tricks-of-the-trade, no structure, no paint qualities, no impasto, no plasticity, no relationships, no experiments, no rules, no coercion, no anarchy, no anti-intellectualism, no irresponsibility, no innocence, no irrationalism, no low level of consciousness, no nature-mending, no reality-reducing, no life-mirroring, no abstracting from anything, no nonsense, no involvements, no confusing painting with everything that is not painting."

I have not quoted any of these artists to ridicule them, nor as a reflection on their work. For it must be again said that a poor philosopher may be a fine painter. And again that Expressionism charged with life has more beauty in it than a morally legalized, philosophically valid, scrupulously honest Grade A copy of a lived experience, which is dead as doornails. But I wish to indicate the loose thinking, the debased critical standards, the apparent chaos, despair, defeatism and frustration which have fallen over much of the current art thinking in America, as in Europe. This want of hard horse sense, the total lack of earthy humor, the absence of the old American relish for the noisy, buoyant, vulgar, romantic, tender, episodic qualities in life, is hardly consistent with our tradition. What is the explanation?

Johann Wolfgang von Goethe published his *Sorrows of Werther* in 1774 and Jean Jacques Rousseau his *Confessions* fourteen years later. These two books ushered in the Romantic Movement and the subjective, expressionist approach in art and literature. For Expressionism, unlike Cubism, is the extreme phase of the Romantic Movement, *le dernier mot,* the last gasp.

I believe, however, that although the extreme Expressionism of the hour is in no sense an organic element of the Modern Movement — of the search for a new faith — yet it does express the uncertainty, the hopelessness, the moral despair of a tortured world, which has drifted from its moorings and found no anchorage to which it can cling. In this sense, it is the negative, defeatist, backward-looking protest of contemporary art. This is what Somerset Maugham means when he says that since "liberty throughout the world is dead . . . artists have not yet learned how to deal with what really matters and so are driven to devote themselves to decorations and spiritual kickshaws." Enzo Paci is right in saying that extreme Expressionism is the inarticulate cry of anarchical freedom; and that, on the other hand, the experiments in abstract formalism are a desperate search for a world with a new significance. The ever-wider gulf between chaotic freedom and a cold, abstract, and intellectual order, detached from the lived realities, the warm and throbbing core of life, points to the failure of our age to strike a balance between freedom and order. And one must conclude with Malraux that art today is questioning a civilization to which it no longer belongs.

15'

MODERNISM:
CONTENT AND FORM

From the Author's Diary, January 26, 1952. The wise artist burrows among the treasures of the past not just for the sensuous enjoyment of some particular treasure but — like the early robin on the lawn — in search of that particular nourishment which at the moment his appetite instinctively demands for his creative growth. And perhaps wisely he rejects, unlike the mere amateur, every form of nourishment which his creative instinct cannot assimilate.

I remember my friend Frederick Frieseke, who used color as delicately fragile as a butterfly's wing, but who had little sense of plastic form, once saying to me with his innocently dogmatic finality that he had never seen any particle of beauty in Hellenic sculpture. In my own development, until my eyes were opened through long talks with Hunt Diederich and Gaston Lachaise and before I devoted two years to modeling and carving in wood and stone, I was equally irresponsive to plastic form. It was not until my first year in Italy in 1932 that I was moved by the grave and measured counterpoint of Piero's compositions. And although at that time I felt that the mosaics at Monreale in Palermo were among the seven wonders of the world, it has only been during these past few months in Rome that there burst upon me for the first time all the masculine vigor and transcendent nobility of Byzantine art.

Byzantium and the Renaissance: ideal or visual truth, the inner or the outer world, the introverted or the extroverted expression of life? In all great art there is both. It is of course a question of degree and emphasis. So, too, is that other closely related problem which today vexes so many of us, the relation of subject matter, form — line, color, and design — and content, the artist's creative message.

Recently I have been reading Lionello Venturi's La Peinture. Although his terminology is somewhat different from mine, he feels the way I do — the way Ozenfant, another early protagonist of Modern Art, feels — that neither subject matter nor plastic form has in itself any ultimate significance, but is *merely part of the sum total which constitutes the content, the artist's imaginative response to his surroundings.**

During the past fifty years, a world period of scientific preoccupation in every branch of human endeavor, the techniques have expanded far more rapidly than have our intelligent use of them. People will generally agree that the scientific concepts upon which nuclear fission is based have far more logic and beauty than the use to which the atom bomb was first put in Japan. For techniques — technical inventions — are only the means to an end. This is as true in art as in science or any other expression of civilization. It is not unnatural that in music, literature, art, and architecture, the excitement in the new techniques and the new art forms created by them should outrun the interest in the artistic message. Time and again artist and critic alike have confused the essence of art, which deals with life and is imagination, with technical ingenuity and stylistic novelty. But this confusion of art and artistry may become a threat to the life of art itself, to painting and sculpture in the grand tradition of our Western inheritance.

Art and artistry, content and form, are so closely integrated that they sometimes, as in the greatest works of art, merge into one harmonious expression. That is why it is often difficult to distinguish one from the other. Could anyone say with assurance, for instance, that Claude Monet's use of the divided color stroke, Manet's insistence on painting his sitters in a flat outdoor light, as they actually appear to us, rather than in an artificial studio lighting, Cézanne's technique of laboriously building up his forms in pseudo-geometric planes, or the various technical devices of the Cubists and abstractionists, are not essentially part of their unique and responsive vision of life? If one must draw the line between content and

---

* "L'important, c'est la contribution humaine qu'une peinture nous offre, ses suggestions à notre façon de sentir et à notre imagination . . .

"[Notre système de critique] est fondé sur la distinction entre le sujet et le contenu, et sur l'identité du contenu et de la forme . . . Le sujet, c'est ce que le peintre a représenté. Mais le contenu, c'est *comment* il l'a représenté . . . Les 'valeurs plastiques' n'existent pas. Ce qui existe, c'est la valeur du rapport entre la plastique et l'imagination du peintre qui a créé l'effet plastique.

"Detacher le sujet, le contenu ou les éléments physiques de la forme — ligne, relief, couleur — de l'ensemble de la peinture, signifie négliger sa valeur d'art . . .

"Une ligne, un effet plastique, une harmonie de couleurs n'ont pas autre chose qu'une valeur technique tant que l'imagination n'y a pas imprimé la passion, le contenu individuel de l'artiste" (Venturi, in *La Peinture*).

form it will sometimes seem arbitrary. But on account of the possible confusion one must always bear in mind that there is a difference, a difference as real as that between strategy and tactics; between gunpowder and the rifling of the barrel.

Mulling over this question recently, I had in mind two contrasting passages in literary criticism. The first was that famous dictum of Poe's in his essay on the "Poetical Principle," in which he states that lyric poetry must by its nature and definition be short. He argues that one can only sustain the poetic emotion for a brief moment; a long poem ceases to be poetic. The other passage is from an article by Somerset Maugham on Balzac. In it he writes: "It is odd that the four greatest novelists the world has known (Balzac, Tolstoi, Dostoevski and Dickens) should have written their respective languages so ill. It looks as though to write well were not the essential part of the novelist's equipment, but that vigor and vitality, imagination, creative force, observation, knowledge of human nature, with an interest in it and sympathy with it, are all more important. All the same," he concludes, "it is better to write well than badly."

Which of these two critics is the more sound: Poe, who argues that the length of a lyric poem determines its artistic quality, or Maugham, who suggests that good writing is not essential to a great novel? Both of course can be right, for Poe had in mind the form of a poem and Maugham the content of a novel.

It struck me that word for word what Maugham said about novels is also true of great paintings. But the interesting thing in the passage is that perhaps without intention he defines in the clearest terms the difference between art and artistry. Contrasting these two passages it occurred to me that in gauging the creative excellence of painting we invariably have one of two standards in mind, neither of which has anything to do with the other: on the one hand, creative insight or imaginative depth, qualities concerned with the drama or interpretation of life; on the other hand, inventiveness or ingenuity, qualities primarily concerned with artistry, technical experimentation, and proficiency. Let me cite a few examples which will more or less illustrate my point. In the field of painting, Goya, Blake, Corot, Homer and Ryder show no spectacular innovations. They speak in an idiom which they have found complete and satisfying for what they have to say. And although they stretch their idiom occasionally and add a word or two when needed, they are primarily concerned, not only in telling a story through the combination and selection of the plastic words with which they present it, but more especially in evoking an emotion or mood by the telling. But they are not particularly concerned in altering the usual meaning of words or the accepted rules of syntax.

Rembrandt's famous "Night Watch" is a dramatic example of the point I am trying to make. Although this painting showed no particular technical innovations, yet on account of its dramatic insight and presentation it perhaps became the turning point in the artist's career and the source of inspiration to other painters for generations. At the age of twenty-six this gifted and precocious artist had already a full command of his technique. At this time he painted the "Anatomy Lesson," a brilliantly executed but somewhat conventional group portrait, a genre much in vogue at the time. Such was its immediate success that his fame seemed assured. Commissions poured in, and the young artist found himself overnight affluent and fashionable. Ten years later, using the same technique, he painted the "Night Watch" (Fig. 19), a similar portrait group commission. But by selecting for the presentation of his sitters that moment when the burgher company turned out of their quarters to some parade or shooting contest, he was able to mass his sitters in the dramatic lighting which he used from then on so effectively to reflect his own shadowy, profound, and grandiose vision. His commissioners, however, were dissatisfied with the unconventional approach. From then on Rembrandt received fewer and fewer portrait orders and some twenty-odd years later he died almost forgotten and in deep poverty.

Albert Ryder is another example of an inspired and influential artist who used the traditional style with which to express the bold sweep of his imagination. Critics have quite rightly pointed out that he anticipated modern design in the sheer and powerful abstractions in which he phrased the masses of his lights and shadows. I don't think they have ever sufficiently made clear that in creating these abstractions he used much the same techniques and color palette as the great Swiss Romanticist Boecklin; and that he evoked a literary mood far closer to that of Sir Walter Scott than of Gertrude Stein or Guillaume Apollinaire.

In appraising Rembrandt's "Night Watch" we are moved by his imaginative insight, dramatic feeling, and interpretation of character. The painting has mirrored the background and culture from which he developed. More than that, to paraphrase Malraux, it is the question mark with which the artist confronts our universe.* For we are dealing, not with a technique, but an explosive life force. On the other hand, Rembrandt, in the field of etching, and Goya, in the field of lithography, because they found it essential to their creative expression, experimented and improved the techniques of these media to such an extent that we almost think of their having invented them! A great inventor's technique and phrasing can sometimes be imitated by lesser academic simians with manual dexterity. But no human being has ever successfully counterfeited a great artist's vision of what life meant to him.

One has in mind, too, the Italian artists of the Renaissance, Michelangelo, Leonardo, Piero della Francesca, Mantegna and Signorelli, who showed a similar intellectual preoccupation in their technical experimentations with anatomical research and linear perspective. But into these new techniques they poured an excitement about life which gave the Renaissance vitality for five centuries. Toward the end of the Middle Ages, in the field of music, a similar technical experimentation occurred in the development of counterpoint and the fugue. One example of such experimentation was the "crab" construction, as it was called, compositions that could be played backwards. Used by the great masters this musical form was capable of rich development. In the hands of uninspired craftsmen it became a meaningless technical *tour de force*.

During the summer of 1928 I went on a sketching trip to Tehuantepec with Diego Rivera, that inspired, romantic, uncouth and often unscrupulous character. His unquestioned genius — apart from half a dozen really great mural panels — lies in his conception of what art can be, when it is once more elevated from the level of the easel, the art dealer and the private collector, to that of a national cultural expression enjoyed by every grade of society. One would suppose that he, more than

---

* "C'est contre [le XX siècle] que tente de se constituer, à tatons, *le premier humanisme universel* . . . Comme les sciences, [notre civilisation] est interrogative, et notre art, lui aussi, devient une interrogation du monde . . . Tout art . . . suggère de plus en plus la mise en question d'un monde qui n'est pas le sien" (Malraux, *La Psychologie de l'art*).

others, understood the difference between art and ingenuity. Yet all of us have our own little jealousies and hurt feelings that sometimes cloud our understanding.

"It was I who invented the guitar motif," Rivera confided to me one day; "Picasso admitted to me that he had stolen it." He was seated, brush in hand, on a small camp stool, his pistol and sombrero rather than his watercolor the focus of attention of Indian small fry that clustered around in silent and apathetic attention.

I asked, "And just how did Picasso excuse himself?"

"Picasso answered me: 'You and many others have stolen my ideas. In art one has a perfect right to steal all one can. The guitar is only important on account of what I have done with it.'"

Most of Rivera's stories are cut out of whole cloth. But he has a lively imagination, and in time they become legendary. In thinking about this many years later I recalled what Jean Baptiste Camille Corot felt about leaning too heavily on the techniques of other painters. "Be guided by feeling alone," he wrote. "We are only simple mortals, subject to error; so listen to the advice of others, but follow only what you understand and can unite in your own feeling. Be firm, be meek, but follow your own convictions. It is better to be nothing than an echo of other painters. The wise man has said: When one follows another, one is always behind. Beauty in art is truth, bathed in an impression received from nature."

Always the artist employs the appropriate techniques with which to express the content of his vision of life. Although we think of each intuitive response to life as having one particular art form which best expresses it, yet sometimes, if it suits his purpose, the artist may legitimately use a medium which combines the different art forms — the opera or ballet, for example. And it is equally true that sometimes he also legitimately communicates his vision in a medium generally intended for a quite different kind of response. Contemporary criticism, which lays far too much emphasis on the importance or originality of the technique and even more on the purity of the art form, is often sadly irresponsive to the imaginative insight, the only thing in final analysis that can matter. One example of this will make my position clear, although few, I am afraid, will concur with me. It is the portrait work of Jo Davidson.

All will agree, even his most contemptuous disparagers, that Jo Davidson had a rare and penetrating gift of portraiture. And I think they will admit that, although they may prefer the work of other sculptors, many of his own portrait busts could not, even technically, be altered for the better. And they will add with scornful finality: "But it is not sculpture." And it is true that Davidson had little sense of plastic form. When he modeled anything but a human face, his limitations were obvious. His small nudes, his compositions, and his experiments in ceramics are without distinction or personality, often immature, weak, and insensitive. But he had the technique needed to communicate his particular concern, which was of course his "observation, knowledge of human nature, with an interest in it and sympathy with it." For these are the qualities of imagination that in the long run will appeal to the greatest numbers in the audience. And was not his imagination in his chosen field as profound as that of some of those painters who expend their ingenuity in matching white upon white, or arranging squares within squares, or fastidiously dripping paint from containers, or dropping matchsticks or sand or what-not into their avant-gardist *pot au feu*?

"But it is not sculpture."

I have two answers to that. Funk and Wagnalls' *College Standard Dictionary* defines "sculpture" as: "The art of fashioning figures of stone, wood, clay, or metal." And secondly: So what? It may not be sculpture. But it is art — I am again relying on Funk and Wagnalls: "The skillful and systematic arrangement or adaptation of means for the attainment of some end."

At all times great artists have made important technical contributions in their various media of expression. A hundred years ago the French Impressionists integrated their palette and vision with the optical experiments of American physicists. The Paris School, which reached maturity in the great Cubist Exhibition of 1912, was, like its predecessor, Impressionism, a dynamic fermentation of technical exploration. Impressionism explored the laws governing light; Modernism examined the anatomy of design. Each broke with the past, the one with color and studio lighting, the other with the pseudo-classical design and the realistic presentation of the visual world. No wonder that the critics of these movements began to lay more and more emphasis in their writing on technical inventiveness, until little by little they began to appraise a work of art entirely on this basis. I remember with what excitement, as an art student in 1912, I read Théodore Duret's *Peintres impressionistes*, Paul Signac's *D'Eugène Delacroix au Neo-impressionisme*, Albert Gleizes' and Jean Metzinger's *Du Cubisme*, and later on Julius Meier-Graefe's monumental work. Here was amplified in terms of technical innovations step by step the development of an idea, the Modern Movement. Each creative artist, brick upon brick, added his own technical quota to the growing edifice. From Constable to Turner, to Delacroix, to Pissarro, to Manet, to Monet, to Seurat, to Cézanne, the edifice culminated in Modernism.

More and more, then, during the past fifty years the most intelligent and progressive art criticism has concerned itself with technical innovations, the development of a movement, a new plastic or pictorial idiom, with the battle between the reactionary and modern schools. Nor was there anything improper in this approach as long as critic and public realized that the discussion was not concerned with appraising the unique and intuitive insight of the individual artist, but with analyzing the development of a historical movement in art, in authenticating an international style.

This does not mean that specific artists or works of art have been neglected by this field of criticism. But more and more they were appraised on the basis of technical innovations, and today almost never on the far more important basis of their vitality, imagination, "observation and knowledge of human nature with an interest in it and sympathy with it." How could one intelligently discuss in these terms the abstractions of Léger, Mondrian, Braque, Picasso, Arp or Miró? So confused has the distinction become between imagination and technical innovation, between creative insight and style, that recently, in commenting on a large portrait group by Raphael Soyer, the art critic of *The New York Times* suggested that the painting "suffers somewhat from the individualization of portraits . . . [the artist's] chief fault, I have always felt, being his primary involvement with his subject matter." As if Shakespeare or Tolstoi or Michelangelo were not involved with the characters they created!

Aleksandr Porfirievich Archipenko, a leading modernist, who has "rejected Cubism in his attempt to obtain pure, abstract sculpture," writes in the catalogue of a recent exhibition of his work: "Following my way of inventions in sculpture, I now use the conductivity of light in plastic. This success in modeling light has come after much experimentation. The plastic works in this exhibition consist of four esthetic elements — first, modeling of space; second, concave; third, transparency; and, as the fourth element, the modeling of light effected by electricity." Leonardo da Vinci once wrote: "A good painter is to paint two things, namely man and the workings of a man's mind. The first is easy, the second difficult." Archipenko is chiefly interested in technical experimentation. Leonardo was obsessed with the interpretation of spiritual life.

16'

SOME LESSER ISMS; RECAPITULATION

Daniel Cory, "Santayana's Last Year," Atlantic Monthly, April 1953: Day by day he grew weaker and weaker. Frequently I would find him asleep, or under the influence of an injection of morphine. But there were a few lucid intervals in the sad gray grimness of waiting for the final release.

One afternoon, about five days before he died, I found him awake and for the moment free from pain. I urged him not to talk if it would tire him, but he said there were a few things he would like to remind me of while there was still time.

"There is, on the one hand," he began, "the natural world which can be partly traced by science with its methods of controlled observation. But there is also the other world — the mosaic of the imagination — which I personally like best. The important thing to remember, however, is not to drown yourself in either of these worlds. They are both essential for any philosophy digne de son nom.

"Always bear in mind," Santayana continued, "that my naturalism does not exclude religion; on the contrary, it allows for it. I mean that religion is the natural reaction of the imagination when confronted by the difficulties of a truculent world. . .

"What I have all my life yearned for is not unity, but completion. If I see a circle half-drawn, I yearn to complete it."

Modern Art is perhaps the least well understood phase of the revolution which since its eruption in 1914 has been reshaping civilization and altering the pattern of our world. Curiously enough, the artistic has been less objectively studied than the military, the economic, the scientific and the nationalistic phases of the same universal upheaval. These other expressions of the Modern Movement — the imperfectly outlined civilization of tomorrow — have more deeply affected the lives of men and nations, and yet, with the exception of science, they are less clearly defined than are the generally admitted characteristics of Modern Design. This is all the more curious in that — again with the exception of science — Modern Design is the only expression of our age which has been universally and complaisantly accepted by the general public.

Although the layman has accepted modern design as the appropriate style for the new age, he is bewildered and often angered by the manifestoes of the artists. The joyful clowning of the Dadaists and Surrealists, the heated asseverations of the Cubists, Futurists, Vorticists, Neoplasticists and Constructivists, and the doubletalk and meaningless jargon of some of the popular highbrow art critics have not always been helpful.

Modernism had its origin in Paris. The tremendous creative fertility of Paris is partly due — as was the case in ancient Athens — to the passionate intellectual hair-splitting which it seemed to live on. Such dialectic controversy is apt to accompany any great radical movement. It may be asked, however, why in my analysis of Modern Art I have placed such emphasis on Abstraction and Expressionism to the exclusion of many of the other "isms" which must be classed under the movement.

Cubism, Futurism, Vorticism, Purism,* Neoplasticism, and Constructivism were essentially different phases of the fundamental search and compulsive drive of the Modern Movement, in every field of art, for a new formal design — or idiom — in which it could express its reaction to a new world. All of these mushroom schools were distinguished by those specific elements of design and their structural relations which characterize Modern Design. They have been adequately treated by such scholarly critics and participants as Ozenfant, Gleizes, André Salmon, Maurice Raynal, Waldemar-George, Lionello Venturi, Alfred Barr and others.

Dadaism, on the contrary, the "Big No," the credo of anarchism, of negativisim, of the noisy, obstructionist frustration of the European intelligentsia of World War I, is closely akin to some of the extreme forms of Expressionism today. It had, however, one little touch of forgivable hypocrisy, which marks it off from the threshold of lunacy. Intended for the delectation of a sophisticated audience, it always held its tongue in its

---

* "Machines are healthy and present an implacable something that stirs us. Fernand Léger was moved by the terrific mechanism of modern war and the precision of objects such as cannons, bombs, weapons: he realized the chronometric rigorousness that sets in motion the thousand cogs of war . . . He was ripe for the appreciation of Purist conceptions" (Amédée Ozenfant, on Purism, in *Foundations of Modern Art*).

cheek. It belonged rather in the realm of philosophic clowning than to the tragic and genuine despair of one of Kafka's novels or a self-portrait by Van Gogh.

Surrealism, which, judging by its accomplishment, is the most fertile as well as the least ephemeral of these various offspring of Modernism, is perhaps the most difficult to classify. Its affinity to the paintings of Brueghel the Elder and Hieronymus Bosch has of course been recognized. The emotive inspiration is different. The sixteenth-century Flemish artists clothed their protests against the censorship of the Counter Reformation in a language of allegories. The Surrealists today voice their escape from reality through the symbolism of psychoanalysis and the subconscious dream world.* The larger truth to bear in mind is that Surrealism is fancy. Fancy is imagination. Imagination is the cornerstone of Modernism — as also the common denominator which unites its many different phases. Every art has had its Surrealists — the paintings of Bosch, *Alice in Wonderland,* the *Lonely Ones* of Bill Steig, the cartoons of Charles Addams and much of Walt Disney at his best. Under the imagery lies buried some reflective grain of criticism — conscious or unconscious — of our world.

Surrealism, although a far more serious manifestation of Modern Art than Dadaism, has in it some of the quality of dead-pan nonsense which distinguished the earlier movement. In the spring of 1941 I attended the opening, at Frank Perl's Gallery in Hollywood, of Man Ray, one of the early Surrealists. He was indeed perhaps the only American who, quite on his own, successfully crashed the Maginot Line of the inner art world of the Ecole de Paris. I remember having first met him twenty years before when I was living with Hunt Diederich at 40½ Barrow Street in Greenwich Village. I had been much impressed by the large, dark, troubled, wistful eyes; the delicately chiseled, ascetic Iberian

---

* "The man himself [Paul Klee] the Surrealists took to their bosoms; they also admired Odilon Redon and the aged James Ensor. The art they desired was to be perceptible subliminally. And indeed mystic spiders, the most esoteric fishes in the Prince of Monaco's collections, the enchanted or 'macabre' islands of Boecklin, ancient and naive treatises on anatomy dating from the Renaissance or Descartes, strange flowers, crawling and parasitic creatures, butterfly-fish, even Wagnerian flower-females, illumine a universe less ethereal than may seem from the reading of their theories . . . I have always defined the object of art as the easing of the pain of reality, the helping us to EVADE reality. It is that same aim and terminology which the doctrinnaires of Surrealism have adopted as their own" (Ozenfant, *Foundations of Modern Art*).

face; the gently modulated voice; and the slow, deliberate gestures. Later I occasionally saw him in Paris with Kiki or Marcel Duchamp at the Dôme. Duchamp at the moment had given up painting for chess. Man Ray had become a successful photographer. I was always impressed by the clear cool intelligence which seemed lurking behind the extravagance of his art theories. Nor could I ever detect any perceptible relation between the whimsy of his paintings and his very fine, traditional portrait photography. Here again in California he was still quite seriously uttering with his charming gravity the pompous and irascible nonsense of the French Dadaists of 1916. In his catalogue he wrote:

"Man Ray has no problems and he does not propound any. The problems are already solved when he presents his work. . .

"It suffices for Man Ray to be confronted with any law of man or nature, to feel an irresistible desire to violate that law. . .

"Man Ray has always been reluctant to expose his work to contemporary opinion; he himself is sure only of his works of twenty years ago, which, in a single lifetime, is the equivalent of centuries of collective judgment. . .

"And so he presents a few of his older works with confidence; and some of his most recent in a spirit of provocation."

Later that spring I undertook an ambitious portrait of Man Ray. I have from time to time enjoyed painting intimate friends or fellow artists in some informal setting which would offer the proper background for the interpretation of their inner spirit. Man Ray has a sensitive and distinguished face, aristocratic and a little medieval. He might have sat to El Greco as the model for any one of that beautiful series of Christ's disciples now hanging in the painter's house in Toledo.

Man was enthusiastic about my suggestion for incorporating in the picture a series of Surrealistic emblems as the proper *mise en scène*. I posed him at one end of a small sofa. Behind him hung one of his early abstractions of "Leda and the Swan." At his feet were scattered a number of pages from an illustrated publication of his — *Cahiers de mains de Man Ray*, I think it was called. On the sofa beside him was a still-life arrangement of white cloth, which two small kittens — also included in the composition — were continually pulling to the floor. But the *pièce de résistance* was an enormous horse's skull which I had borrowed from the Los

Angeles County Museum. I had gotten these various props together with no particular interest in their hidden symbolism. One day Man Ray asked me:

"Did you realize the significance of the horse's skull? André Breton, the founder of our movement, at one time was in the National Gallery in London studying Holbein's 'Ambassadors,' which he had always particularly admired. He had never been able to make out the identity of the long object in the lower corner of the painting. Getting down on his hands and knees he looked at it from one side, foreshortened. It was a skull — *hohles Bein* — the painter's signature! That is why the horse's skull has always had symbolic significance in Surrealistic painting."

For several days I searched the Santa Monica beach without success for some gnarled, salt-weathered piñon root to fill in an empty spot in the background of my composition. We both remembered having seen one in the vestibule of the house of Walter Arensberg, whose superb collection of modern French art we had both visited. Arensberg was delighted to let me have this last necessary prop for my Surrealist *décor*. I brought it to my studio, but it turned out to be large and unwieldy. I broke off a foot or two from the stump for greater convenience. I am sorry to say that thereafter my hitherto cordial relations with Walter were never quite the same. I don't just remember how he heard about it, but I cannot forget the sepulchral gravity with which Man said to me: "It is not just that he feels that you have mutilated one of the finest pieces in his collection. What troubles him even more is your insensitivity as an artist. I would suggest that you return him the pieces in their present condition. It would be wiser not to make any attempt to repair the break by gluing the fragments together."

The wealth and importance of the Arensberg collection is too well-known to comment on. He once told me that he was not particularly interested in — or even aware of — the element of design in any of the early French Modernists — Duchamp, Braque, Picasso, Léger, and so on. The only quality which interested him was the psychological symbolism of these paintings. I was too dazed to answer.

I have mentioned this incident because it illustrates some of the complexities and contradictions of Modernism. The artists that joined together in that movement were motivated in different ways. Strong "literary" compulsions may have helped to create the coldest abstraction. Much painting that was intended as an exercise in pure form may have been given ulterior meaning and significance.

In the foregoing pages my basic assumption has been that in its every manifestation: Art is an imaginative reaction to life, expressed in some definite design or rhythm.

For purposes of clarification I have drawn a sharp distinction between the Modern Movement, Modern Design, and Modern Art. This distinction has hitherto never been explicitly dwelt upon, which is one reason for much of the contemporary misunderstanding and cat-calling.

I have defined the Modern Movement as our New World and its manifestation in every sphere of human thought and activity — ethical, political, scientific, esthetic. I have defined Modern Design as the new idiom or language of every art form — music, painting, sculpture, architecture, literature or the ballet — in which the Modern Movement is gropingly attempting to express itself. And lastly I have distinguished Modern Art as the intuitive creative expression of the Modern Movement, what it has to say — presumably in the new idiom, but essentially in any style or mingling of styles which best expresses its meaning.

I have suggested that in the survey of art from the earliest times and in every known civilization the basic elements of design seem roughly to group themselves into one of two major stylistic approaches in design. And further that the culture which each style represents seems to have certain traits and attitudes toward life — the extroverted and introverted — which are more or less consonant, and appropriately expressed by the graphic elements and the characteristics of such style.

Part III • Contemporary Trends

AMERICAN ART OVER
FIFTY YEARS

From the Author's Diary, January 28, 1949. I again visited the exhibition of 100 Paintings of the 20th Century currently shown at the Metropolitan Museum. My portrait of Marguerite Zorach, painted in 1934, doesn't show up too badly, although I wish the Museum had owned a more recent and characteristic example of my work. This is the most provocative exhibition of American art ever gotten together in this country. It has attempted to bring together examples of the work of the most important American painters of the past fifty years, but also to indicate the various schools of art embraced in this period. More than ever it has thrust home the need of some yardstick of appraisal with which to judge these so different trends. Again one is aware of the prodigious technical advances that have taken place in painting — as of course also in sculpture, music, architecture and poetry — between the horse-and-buggy and the atomic age. Yet I wonder if there is not almost as great a difference in the character of the message which these artists are trying to make clear with their diverse techniques.

The forty deceased artists include Whistler, Ryder, Homer, Eakins and Mary Cassatt, all of whom were born in the thirties and forties of the past century, so that the showing covers very nearly a hundred years of American painting. Here are hung the works of Remington, Abbey and John Sargent, together with the works of the Ashcan School, the rebels of their day. And alongside these earlier artists are shown our contemporary painters: traditionalists, realists, modernists, and nonobjectivists. Is Stamos, Baziotes, Pollock, De Kooning, Feininger, Tobey or Rattner a greater artist than Ryder, Blakelock, Mary Cassatt, Abbey, Sargent or Remington? Who has the more completely mirrored his age? Who has the more original imagination and the more profound message to relate? Which one a hundred years from now will the more completely live? And why?

These are some of the questions which this exhibition has raised for me. By what values shall we create a standard of criticism to determine our appraisal? Here lies the problem which artist and critic and layman alike must

*face. It is not enough to say that we prefer the extreme traditional and realistic,
or the middle-of-the-road modern, or the avant-gardists of Expressionism and
nonobjective art. We must ask ourselves on what affirmation of belief our
preference rests.*

Since 1900 much water has spilled over the dam. Perhaps there is no
half-century recorded in history in which so many portentous events
have happened. In that year Queen Victoria was still alive. *Main Street*
would not be published for another twenty-one years. Edna St. Vincent
Millay was an eight-year-old schoolgirl in Rockland, Maine. Duveneck
and Chase had received their art education in Germany. The transfer of
allegiance of American art from Munich and Dusseldorf to Paris was still
viewed with suspicion by the academies. And although Childe Hassam
and Mary Cassatt exhibited at the Pennsylvania Academy annual — the
leading art event of the season — the tone was set by the society portraits
of such painters as Sargent, Chase, Cecilia Beaux, Howard Cushing,
George de Forest Brush and John White Alexander. Yet at the turn of
the century, or shortly thereafter, several of our contemporary Americans were working in Paris: John Marin, Maurice Sterne, Max Weber,
Abraham Walkowitz; and a little later, William and Marguerite Zorach.

Fashions change. So much can happen in a lifetime. For the purpose,
then, of seeing the present, postwar art trend in its proper perspective,
let us briefly glance at these successive movements since the turn of the
century.

The significance of the Ashcan School was not related to any particular esthetic philosophy or technique, nor with the ambition of found-
ing a new school in painting. Rather it was one of the recurrent swings of
the pendulum away from the prevalent academic studio art — nudes, still
lifes and official portraits — and toward a reaffirmation of human values.
It is perhaps a coincidence that Henri, Glackens, Luks and Shinn all
studied under Anschutz, who inherited Thomas Eakins' mantle at the
Pennsylvania Academy. It is more than a coincidence that, like Winslow
Homer forty years earlier, they had all begun their careers as reporter-
illustrators, in this instance on Philadelphia newspapers. The Ashcan
School, then, was a reëmphasis on the human content in art; as American
as Grandma Moses or Currier and Ives, as universal as Daumier or Kathe
Kollwitz.

Then like a crash came the Armory Exhibition of 1913. For months all of New York went to see the cause of the hullabaloo, and there were full-page reproductions in papers and journals from Waco to Kalamazoo, from New York to Sacramento. One recalls the flutter and chatter over Marcel Duchamp's "Le Nu descendant l'escalier" and "Un Roi vite." Post-Impressionism, Neo-Impressionism, Cubism, Futurism; Lehmbruck, Modigliani, Matisse, Picasso, culminating in more or less logical sequence from Courbet, Manet, Renoir, Gauguin, Van Gogh and Cézanne. All this was for the first time seen by the great American public. They saw it, discussed it, thoroughly disliked it, and did not entirely forget it.

But it was different with the artists. The exhibition had a vitalizing influence on the creative impulse in America. It had been organized by American painters, under the leadership of Arthur B. Davies and Walt Kuhn; and many contemporary Americans were included. Not only was the Armory Show the choice and expression of the younger, radical, and more intellectually minded painters, but it had the effect of fusing them into a self-conscious group, very much alive to the international movement which flamed in Paris before World War I. Hitherto some of these artists — I was one among them — had individually studied the movement in Paris, or to a minor degree been part of it. But after 1913 they were conscious of themselves as forming a group of modern American artists.

During the next few years there slowly banded together a smallish group of painters, sculptors and designers who avidly studied French art. Max Weber (Fig. 9) had been in Matisse's atelier. Pascin, Hunt Diederich and Eli Nadelman were to some extent known in Paris already. Generally speaking the work of this younger group was not exhibited by museums or galleries. It was natural, then, in their intransigence, that their art was often ingrown, self-searching, probing of esthetic problems. A swing toward Paris, African sculpture, Hopi Indian design, and abstraction characterized this period. Sentimentality, the academic outlook, realism, tradition and John Singer Sargent were anathema. As Constantin Brancusi summed up this attitude to me: "Michelange et Rodin: c'est du biftek." (What he meant by "biftek" was cornmeal mush.) Davies, by some acclaimed the father of the group, covered his Celtic moonlight romanticism with a filmy netting of cubism. It was a moment of rebellion, youth, daring, inconsistency and faith.

The Modernists of 1913 and the following years were swinging away from the "human interest" note of Luks, Henri, Glackens and Bellows; and they would not willingly have exhibited with these rebels of an earlier decade. A few of the names which distinguished the new group were Rockwell Kent, Hunt Diederich, Gaston Lachaise, William and Marguerite Zorach, John Marin, Paul Burlin, Yasuo Kuniyoshi, Joseph Stella, Georgia O'Keeffe, Charles Sheeler, Charles Demuth, Marsden Hartley and Louis Bouché.

The next swing of the pendulum, away from French art and esthetic preoccupation with formal design, was precipitated by the depression years. The Great Depression of the 1930's perhaps exerted as strong an influence on American art as any other single occurrence in our history. This opposite swing assumed three different aspects: Regionalism, the social-conscious impulse, and the mural movement, supported by federal patronage under the various New Deal projects.

I think of Regionalism as an initially wholesome movement, doomed to sterility through the almost blind prejudice and narrow loyalties of the eminent critic, Thomas Craven. Essentially Regionalism was an attempt to shake off an imported French influence, but it was also a revived and healthy interest in our own American background. Craven, however, narrowed his group of Regionalists to three names: Thomas Hart Benton, John Steuart Curry and Grant Wood. Yet all great realists in the history of art — including the Japanese print-makers — Corot, Winslow Homer, Eastman Johnson, the Hudson Valley School and scores of contemporary artists are regionalists almost by definition. For these reasons Regionalism is often given a chauvinistic and somewhat invidious connotation, which it hardly deserves. Today it is definitely in the doghouse.

The other two directions in art that were given their initial impulse during the depression years I have spoken of as the social-conscious school, which used painting as the vehicle for a critique of American life, and the mural movement, the success of which depended almost wholly on federal patronage. Both groups were part of the same recurrent swing away from preoccupation with formal values and toward a deeper concern with the human content of their art.

The influence of Regionalism on our younger artists ended during the prewar years, at about the same time that Congress withdrew its support from what remained of the New Deal legislative program. During the summer of 1943, in conference between House and Senate, the funds were withdrawn from the War Department Art Committee, under which civilian artists had been completing the pictorial record of front-line fighting in Europe and the Pacific. That same week Congress liquidated the Section of Fine Arts and the Graphic Division of the Office of War Information. At the time, as Chairman of the War Department project, I was covering the fighting in North Africa. I recorded somewhat bitterly in my Diary: "I do not think you can quite kill — thus in a moment of political conference jobbery among a few tobacco-spitting Congressmen from the Bible Belt — the most intelligent and generous art program that any warring country ever organized for its artists. Such a program was no isolated phenomenon, but the result of other similar human, democratic, and liberal art projects, which bore fruit in our country in recent years. And these again had emerged from the whole art fabric and tradition in America. This you cannot so easily kill. Still one must make the best of it. Salvage something from the ruins of the Congressmen's spite. Begin building anew. There may still be a few weeks before I shall be ordered home."

I was overly pessimistic. Several years later, during another war in which our country became involved, I was asked, as painter-member of the National Commission of Fine Arts, to consider and appraise the relative merits of half-a-dozen bills introduced in Congress for the creation of some sort of national Bureau of Fine Arts. Senior officers from the Army, Navy and Air Force testified to the need of commissioning civilian artists to make pictorial records of the fighting in Korea! The wheels of the gods grind slowly. One must have patience and faith in one's ideals. And always, even with our Congressmen, a grain of humor.

During the war years, when I was much of the time overseas or in Brazil and Mexico working on mural commissions for the governments of these countries, there occurred another swing of the pendulum, once more away from the "human interest" element in art, away from realism, from subject matter, from social preoccupation, and toward esthetic experimentation with abstract design and the subjective approach. Since there has been much bad temper, intolerance and sloppy thinking in the discussion of current Modernism, it may be pertinent, in an effort to clear the atmosphere and arrive at a common ground of agreement, to make, as objectively as possible, a few observations about this movement.

During the years since World War II, I have not observed among the extreme modernists, either here or in Europe, any technical, esthetic or emotional trend that was not already pretty well established before or immediately after World War I. I can say this with some authority. For I witnessed both the epoch-making Cubist Exhibition in Paris in 1912 and the Armory Show in New York in 1913; and during the three years I spent in Paris between 1923 and 1926 I knew many of the Parisian modernists: Pascin, Duchamp, Zadkine, Chagall, Gleizes, Brancusi, Soutine, Kokoschka, Léger and others. Not, of course, that these painters would be considered avant-gardists today; but actually, I believe, they had pushed their investigations in the realm of color, texture and design — as also in the direction of pure abstraction — to the extreme boundary of technical experimentation. Nor is the "lunatic fringe" of Expressionism today far different in vocal stridency from that of the Dadaism of 1916, which "spat in the eye of the world."

Without, however, showing any important new technical approach in the current postwar abstract or nonobjective movement, its character is distinguishable from the abstract art of the earlier period. I would suggest that generally speaking there is less emphasis on formal design and a greater emphasis on Expressionism and the extreme subjective approach. The line is ever more sharply drawn between the "inarticulate cry of anarchical freedom" and that "stern, bare, and nonhuman construction" trying "desperately for a world of new shapes beyond the natural and human." (Compare Figs. 24, 25 and 26 with Figs. 22, 23.)

I would suggest a further distinction between the two periods. Abstract or nonobjective art has now become academic — I use this word in no invidious sense — in that for at least thirty years it has been accepted as a stylized school of design, a recognized idiom. The movement had matured, had reached its full expression, and had obtained world circulation soon after World War I. For many years now it has received the widest publicity, and during the past decade it has been heavily and snobbishly promoted by every museum in Europe and America. It is generally true that nonobjective art is neither understood nor liked by the general public. But it is not new or radical.

Lastly I would observe that, whether we approve of it or not, extreme abstract and nonobjective painting has a particular appeal to students and to the younger and less conservative art elements of the country. I believe that much of the young creative talent, both here and in Europe, finds its expression in this idiom. I cannot help feeling, then, that the movement fills an emotional need of our times. I am not for the moment attempting an appraisal of its importance, but rather to place it in the context of the other art trends of the past fifty years.

I remember during the winter of 1951 visiting Van Wyck Brooks at Bridgewater, Connecticut, where he had just bought the charming late-Victorian house opposite the two white wooden New England churches and elbow to elbow with the village Grange, the Fire Department, and the one general store and Post Office. He put aside the galley proofs of the fifth volume of his *Makers and Finders, a History of American Literature,* and we talked from lunch time until late in the afternoon. I told him how puzzled and at the same time depressed I had recently felt that the younger contemporary postwar American painting — and European painting, too, as far as I could gather — seemed primarily concerned with the same technical problems and experimentations with which the art world was wrestling just before and after World War I in Paris; whereas, on the other hand, our best younger novelists — Norman Mailer, James Jones, John Hersey, Truman Capote, Irwin Shaw and others — showed a deep concern with contemporary life and human character.

Brooks stressed the difference in literature between contemporary poetry and novel-writing. After the influence of Joyce the novel was brought back to a more acceptable form of communication and a concern with the normal pattern of life. He went on to stress the enormous — and to him malevolent — influence of Ezra Pound and T. S. Eliot in the field of poetry, the uncommunicability of the one and the rejection of traditional American optimism by the other.*

I said: "If that is the case you have suggested a rather close analogy between painting and poetry, for both today seem primarily concerned with an egocentric subjective expression and with the techniques of their respective crafts. I have often wondered whether the much greater financial capital involved in publishing a novel has not had something to do with the difference in approach of writers in the two literary forms.

---

* "[The American character] is the unbreakable tradition that man is the master of his own destiny. Partly it is the faith that there is something unique in America . . . " (Harold Laski, in *American Democracy*).

Where much money is involved books will be written — some of them good and some of them less good — that can be understood by the general public and which deal with problems close to the life of the general public. But less money is involved in the publication of a poem or even in a book of lyrics, and almost any artist can rent a gallery on Fifth Avenue for a few hundred dollars. Nor is lack of proficiency in his craft much of a barrier to an exhibition."

Van Wyck said: "I believe that the problem is more general and profoundly more disquieting. Today the world is in a flux. The fear engendered by war, by insecurity, by revolution has in some sort created a suspension of the creative will. Nor is there either reverence for tradition or standards in art. All this is part of the general world pattern. When Ezra Pound raved against 'Kultur,' he became a powerful force in breaking down the tradition of culture in the field of literature. Pound himself was a scholar, but how many of the young poets have read their classics? I am afraid that art will only emerge," he concluded, "when civilization is once more stabilized."

He was right enough, I felt, in his concern with the breakdown of traditional standards in every field of art; unduly pessimistic, I hope, about the art of the immediate future. But what a lovely, warm, affectionate, and gifted friend! I have known and admired him for almost fifty years, ever since we drank tea together at the Stylus Club at Harvard with Max Perkins, Jack Wheelock, Ned Sheldon and the others.

By and large, then, from the long view it is evident that during this period in painting, in music, in architecture, and in poetry there has been a steady shift away from the traditional modes of expression ushered in by the Renaissance, and also, in much of our painting, literature, and music, away from the curiosity and preoccupation with nature and human life that gave the Renaissance its vitality. Yet within this longer cycle and more slowly moving current can be seen the periodic shorter and more violent fluctuations, ever it would seem, between the same extremes: the extroverted or the introverted approach; the emphasis on the visual and human world or on the preoccupation with formal values; the expression of what is seen outwardly through the eye or inwardly by self-revelation and the mechanically articulated symbols of ultimate truth.

American art today is at the crest of such a recurrent fluctuation between an introverted formalism and the out-looking interest in human beings and curiosity in life. For it is difficult to see how extreme Expressionism can be carried much further than it is and still remain within its accepted formula of paint squeezed, brushed, dripped or poured on masonite or canvas. The search for pure design has progressed from the low-keyed and highly subjective dissonances of the early Cubists to geometric formalism in pure color tones at their highest intensity, or more recently to white squares or rectangles painted on white. Yet many artists working in the Modern medium are beginning to feel that such thin-blooded and fastidious experimentation is becoming the "arbitrary exploitation of a single phase of painting." They have affirmed their belief that "all art is an expression of human experience" and that they should "work to restore to art its freedom and dignity as a living language." *

* The following Statement appeared in 1953 in the first issue of *Reality, A Journal of Artists' Opinions*, signed by forty-seven painters, all of whom, with few exceptions, work in the Modern Idiom: "A group of artists have joined together to discuss their problems. The work of the members of this group is highly diverse in style and conception. Their kinship is a respect and love for the human qualities in painting. The following statement represents their concerted opinion.

"All art is an expression of human experience. All the possibilities of art must be explored to broaden the expression. We nevertheless believe that texture and accident, like color, design and all the other elements of painting, are only the means to a larger end, which is the depicture of man and his world.

"Today, mere textural novelty is being presented by a dominant group of museum officials, dealers, and publicity men as the unique manifestation of the artistic intuition. This arbitrary exploitation of a single phase of painting encourages a contempt for the taste and intelligence of the public. We are asked to believe that art is for the future, that only an inner circle is capable of judging contemporary painting, that everybody else must take it on faith. These theories are fixed in a ritual jargon equally incomprehensible to artist and layman. This jargon is particularly confusing to young artists, many of whom are led to accept the excitation of texture and color as the true end of art, even to equate disorder with creation. The dogmatic repetition of these views has produced in the whole world of art an atmosphere of irresponsibility, snobbery, and ignorance.

"We say, in the words of Delacroix: 'The men of our profession deny to the fabricators of theories the right to thus dabble in our domain and at our expense.' We believe that art cannot become the property of an esoteric cult. We affirm the right of the artist to the control of his profession. We will work to restore to art its freedom and dignity as a living language."

The Statement was signed by Milton Avery, Isabel Bishop, Aaron Bohrod, Louis Bosa, Louis Bouché, Charles Burchfield, Nicolai Cikovsky, Gladys Rockmore Davis, Joseph De Martini, Alexander Dobkin, Guy Pène du Bois, Philip Evergood, Ernest Fiene, Joseph Floch, Xavier Gonzalez, Dorothea Greenbaum, Stephen Greene, William Gropper, Chaim Gross, Maurice Grosser, Robert Gwathmey, Joseph Hirsch, Edward Hopper, Karl Knaths, Leon Kroll, Yasuo Kuniyoshi, Joe Lasker, Sidney Laufman, Jacob Lawrence, Jack Levine, Oronzio Maldarelli, Reginald Marsh, Henry Mattson, Edward Melcarth, Paul Mommer, Sigmund Menkes, Henry Varnum Poor, Anton Refregier, Honoré Sharrer, Joseph Solman, Moses Soyer, Raphael Soyer, William Thon, Anthony Toney, Howard Warshaw, Sol Wilson and Karl Zerbe.

18'

ART AND SOCIETY

From the Author's Diary, November 10, 1948. Six of us from Artists Equity Committee on Museums—Kuniyoshi, Hudson Walker, Henry Poor, Leon Kroll, Eugene Speicher and myself—had dinner with Francis Taylor and Theodore Rousseau, of the Metropolitan Museum, to discuss the possibility of an annual exhibition of American painting to be given by the Museum. It is an exciting opportunity. Could accomplish a great deal to give prestige and dignity to contemporary American art. I believe that much progress was made.

Taylor began by telling us how in 1941, when he organized Art Week, he went down to Washington to present the results of the program to President Roosevelt. That afternoon Lord Lothian, the British Ambassador, had flown in from London. Taylor's appointment was postponed and he waited for two hours while Lord Lothian gave the President the first eye-witness report of the London bombings. When Taylor eventually got in to see him, he found him "white as a sheet." Yet the President kept him in his study for an hour and a half, asking questions and presenting his plans for an eventual popularization of art in America, where "every schoolhouse would have contemporary American paintings hanging on its walls."

Roosevelt had little discrimination in his taste in painting and sculpture. He had a more clear understanding of what art could mean in the life of the community—for the soul of the nation—than any man I have known.

Franklin Roosevelt, in his Dedication Address at the opening of the National Gallery in Washington, March 17, 1941: "There was a time when the people of this country would not have thought that the inheritance of art belongs to them or that they had responsibilities to guard it. A few generations ago the people of this country were taught by their writers and by their critics and by their teachers to believe that art was something foreign to America and to themselves—something imported from another continent and from an age that was not theirs—something they had no part in, save to go to see it in a guarded room on holidays or Sundays.

"But recently, within the last few years, they have discovered that they *have a part. They have seen in their own towns, in their own villages, in schoolhouses, in postoffices, in the back rooms of shops and stores, pictures painted by their sons, their neighbors — people they have known and lived beside and talked to. They have seen, across these last few years, rooms full of paintings by Americans, walls covered with the painting of Americans — some of it good, some of it not good, but all of it native, human, eager and alive — all of it painted by their own kind in their own country, and painted about things they know and look at often and have touched and loved.*

"The people of this country know now, whatever they were taught or thought they knew before, that art is not something just to be owned but something to be made: that it is the act of making and not the act of owning which is art. And knowing this they know also that art is not a treasure in the past or an importation from another country, but part of the present life of all living and creating peoples — all who make and build; and, most of all, the young and vigorous peoples who have made and built our present wide country." *

The significance of Modern Design is that it best expresses the organic meaning and the needs of a new and changing world. Yet Modern Art was created by the intelligentsia of Europe — France, Italy, Germany, the Netherlands and Russia. The French capital was the hub of the artistic life of Europe, and it is not surprising that the movement became known as the Ecole de Paris. It has been, since its inception, an aristocratic art, intended for the initiates, a cultured and sophisticated audience. Here we have an apparent anomaly, frequently repeated in history, of a radical movement originated by the members of an older system or culture whose techniques and creeds the new ideas are destined to supersede.

In the great periods of art, such as the culmination of Gothic culture in the thirteenth century, the artist stood at the center of life. The civilization to which he belonged had a universal faith or religion, which held an identical meaning for peasant, priest or king. And so the artist — Dante or Giotto — in his recreation of the visual world, could give expression in his art to this universality, the wholeness of life, the "completion" of George Santayana's circle.

* The first draft of President Roosevelt's Dedication Address was written at his request by Archibald MacLeish, then Librarian of Congress. The President, however, made a considerable number of changes in the original draft, further last-minute changes in the reading copy, and additional extemporaneous interpolations in the delivery of the address.

During the Middle Ages and later during the Renaissance, art had been commissioned by the church or state to serve a religious or social aim. With few exceptions it has been only during the past three or four hundred years that paintings are collected, bought as art objects with a rising or falling value on the open market, rather than paid for on a commission basis for a service rendered. Gradually with the growth of science and the capitalistic structures, Europe went through a long period of social and economic readjustment. Art was no longer thought of as integrated with the life of the community, and slowly it became more and more divorced from the general public and society.

During these centuries the artist moved from the center to the periphery of life. By the middle of the nineteenth century he often began to think of himself, or was thought of, as an outsider, a rebel, a bohemian. On June 17, 1855, Eugène Delacroix wrote in his *Journal*: "Paris, whose opinion puts the seal on reputations, is composed of five hundred persons who have minds and who judge and think for the mass of two-legged animals who live in Paris, but who are Parisians in name only." Nor has this feeling of isolation from his audience diminished during the intervening years. I remember how I savored the sensation of belonging to a community apart — the aristocratic elite of the world of art — when Frieseke said to me one day at Giverny in 1916 that he would be quite content if there were five or six persons in any large city who understood his painting. That year he had been awarded the Second Medal at the Salon International des Beaux Arts, the highest award ever given a foreigner.

This withdrawal of the artist from the center to the periphery of society * reached its culmination about the time of World War I. The group

* "Perhaps the most conspicuous quality of contemporary art is the extreme loneliness of its author which it reflects. His divorce from society which at first he welcomed has become complete. To visit any one of a score of recent exhibitions leaves the impression one has at looking into the brilliantly illuminated window of a hardware store on a cold winter's night. There we see row upon row of precision instruments, circular saws arranged in geometric patterns, and pneumatic tools wreathed in coils of electric cable; each item, however, is inert and impotent unless it is plugged into the wall to receive the impulse of some source of unseen power. The spectacle is exciting, but it is unrewarding and frustrating.

"Progress and catastrophe. The answer lies in our own hearts rather than our intellects. Standing on the threshold of a new and infinitely more productive world from which national and international suicide is separated by only the thinnest and most fragile membrane, we, who have derived so much from our inherited civilization, are obligated to give it another chance for progress. The artist, then, if he chooses to retain his stature as prophet, must reassert his belief in man" (Francis Henry Taylor, in *The Art Digest*, May 1, 1953).

of artists of which Matisse was the best-known exponent was dubbed "les fauves," the wild beasts. And a subsequent movement proclaimed that the highest function of art was to speak in a meaningless language—the utmost it had to say of life was "Da da da da!" And finally the Surrealists based their philosophy on the supreme significance of the subconscious, of a dream world. This growing tendency of the artist to escape from the life of reason and humanity, from the consideration of ethical standards and his own role as a prophet in the community, is a tragic abandonment of our twin tradition of Hellenic and Christian civilization. The artist, cast out from the society to which he belongs, comes gradually to think of himself as a bohemian, a rebel, a wild beast. He surrenders his function to portray and to criticize life for the opiate of the subconscious dream.

During the years in which Modern Art reached maturity, the artist himself, the creator of this great new language, was escaping further and further from the audience to which he spoke. But meanwhile a new conception of art was slowly developing, having nothing properly to do with esthetics or the new techniques but which might be destined to establish the artist once more nearer to the center of society from which he had too long been banished.

Perhaps the most important art form which the Renaissance revived was the easel painting, important because it gave greater range and flexibility to the subjective approach, as also to the new delight in nature and the human being. And it was the easel painting, bought by the collector, with a rising or falling value on the open market, which more than anything else established the reputation of the artist and gradually became the principal source of his income. It was the wealth of the royalty, the aristocracy, and finally of the bourgeoisie of Europe upon which the livelihood of the artist largely depended; as it was the intelligence and taste of the same groups upon which depended the direction and esthetic excellence of his work.

The recent trend, however, involves a readjustment of the social and economic relation between the artist and the public, a relation which generally speaking has existed since the middle of the seventeenth century. This tendency has resulted to a very great extent in the financing of art—the rationalization of the artist's product—on a different basis. In brief, art is increasingly acquired and paid for as a service; as something having a recreational, educational or social value — as, for instance, a book or a theatre ticket or a piece of furniture is purchased — and not as an *objet d'art* with a speculative value.

This is of course an economic tendency. But economic forces may exert a very great, although an indirect, influence on creative art. And it will be noted that, although at the turn of the century the Paris art world was fluid, radical and vitally creative in the sphere of esthetics, yet in the realm of economics the conception of the marketing of art and the relation of art to society had altered little in three centuries.

The Mexican mural renascence was the first notable example of an important national art expression that did not accompany a rising economic cycle and a wide distribution of private wealth. (See Fig. 27.) Mexican mural art was not financed by private capital but was carried out by the government as a means of educating the masses. It was conceived of, not as a speculative investment, but as a national service. Actually the Mexican mural movement was not the first instance in which nations recognized that art is the greatest emotional vehicle for the education of the masses. In World War I Germany, France, England and the United States mobilized their artists, as mechanically as they mobilized their industries, to sell their respective causes to the home front. In the period between the two wars, Russia, Germany and Italy were perhaps more aware than the democracies of the propagandizing value of art. The exhibitions, the architecture and the music of the totalitarian states were under as strict a national discipline as the youth movements or the five-year plans.

Today all over the world — and very much in America — we see this new, or very old, concept of art manifested in many fields. It was emphatically true under the New Deal Art Relief Projects, in the New Deal mural program to decorate public buildings, and in our army during World War II in the program to make a permanent pictorial record of our combat divisions. We see the same trend in the growing integration of art and industry, where art is used for the first time on a generous scale to advertise business. We observe it in the huge museum attendances, in the growth of "Sunday painters," and in the importance attributed to art in our mass-audience magazines such as *Life* and *Look*. This concept of art as a service has not of course obliterated the other concept of art as a luxury, to be bought on a speculative basis, as diamonds for instance have always been purchased — partly as a source of pleasure, partly as a symbol of "conspicuous consumption," but also as a sound investment in an uncertain capitalistic economy. The two conceptions of art will continue, for both are needed and each fulfills an important role in our civilization. But we cannot sufficiently emphasize the importance of this new — or very old — conception of art as a public service of educational, social, and recreational value to the community.

It was of course the depression of the 1930's which gave the initial impulse in America to this widespread democratization of art. The socially conscious impulse of our artists during these years and the mural movement sponsored by the federal government were both manifestations of this trend. The New Deal Art Projects kept the fires burning in the hearts of over five thousand American artists during several grim winters. But it was not the sustenance to the artists which was the greatest contribution of federal relief. Rather the effect on the nation itself. During these years — and later during the war years — the country became art-conscious as never in its history. In every large city people flocked to the museums. The average annual attendance was over 20,000,000. Five hundred community art centers were organized with an annual attendance of 5,000,-000. The depression was perhaps for all these reasons the strongest and most wholesome influence on American art in our history. In more ways than one it may be said to have marked the end of an era and the beginning of another.

If I venture to make comparisons between the recent democratization of art in America and the status of art among the nations of Europe during the past few centuries, it is not to belittle the culture of Europe, which in general has been on an immeasurably higher level than in the New World, but rather to emphasize the modern channels of mass production — the implications of which have been more readily grasped here than abroad. When the importance of these channels is fully realized by the artist, the critic and the public, all three will appreciate the different social value and, therefore, the different esthetic style and emotional content which a living creative art must have in our contemporary America. It is pure mumbo-jumbo, a meaningless studio jargon, dating from the pastel-colored twilight hours of Whistler and the London esthetes, to assert that an artist only paints to please himself.* He always paints for an audience. The question is: Who constitute the audience?

Walt Disney's cartoon pictures are enjoyed by millions from every social class. Therefore they are drawn in a style which will be understood by those millions; and it is possible to produce them on a mass scale which for many centuries would have been inconceivable anywhere in the world. Since the Renaissance Europe has never had an art audience of any significance outside of the cultured few of its larger cities. Imagine a Fragonard, a Courbet or a Renoir having an immediate and appreciative audience of some fifteen to forty million art lovers. They never had audiences of more than a few thousand, drawn solely from the aristocratic, cultured and privileged classes of the large cities. In using Disney as an example, I am not comparing the quality of his art with that of Renoir. But surely the music of Bach, Beethoven, and Mozart, which is daily enjoyed over the radio by forty to sixty million music lovers, is of as high a standard as that of any art created since the Middle Ages. I use Disney, as I use the classical music radio programs, as dramatic examples of the effect of the mass-production media on the size and democratization of the American audience.

An impartial review of these and similar facts leads us to the conclusion that today in America there is among the general public an ever-widening curiosity and interest in creative art—music, literature, and painting. And it is a truly tragic circumstance that the present expression and product of our artists—although undoubtedly sincere enough and without any question sensitive in technical qualities and in formal phrasing—is so generally lacking in the vitamins and calories capable of satisfying a young and vigorous appetite.

* "I see no need for a community. An artist is always lonely. The artist is a man who functions beyond or ahead of his society. In any case seldom within it. I think our problem would seem to be fundamentally psychological. Some feel badly because they are not accepted by the public. We shouldn't be accepted by the public. As soon as we are accepted, we are no longer artists but decorators. Sometimes we think if we could only explain to the public, they would agree with us. They may agree in the course of years. They won't agree now. . . . they should not agree now. I think this group activity, this gathering together, is a symptom of fear . . . " (David Hare, in *Modern Artists in America*).

18. El Greco. *Burial of Count Orgaz.* Santo Tomé, Toledo

19. Rembrandt. *The Night Watch.* Rijksmuseum, Amsterdam

20. Giovanni Cimabue. *Crucifix.* San Domenico, Arezzo

21. Abraham Rattner. *Among Those Who Stood There.* Paul Rosenberg

22. Fritz Glarner. *Relational Painting.* Museum of Modern Art

23. Robert Motherwell. *Western Air.* Museum of Modern Art

24. Franz Kline. *Chief*. Museum of Modern Art

25. Hans Hofmann. *Ambush*. Museum of Modern
Art

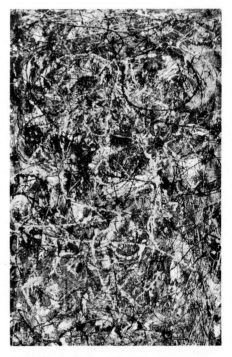

26. Jackson Pollock. *Full Fathom Five*. Museum
of Modern Art

When I speak of a democratic trend, catering to the millions rather than to the sophisticated few, I do not imply a necessary lowering of esthetic standards. That question will solely depend on the talent and integrity of our artists. I do imply an art content which will appeal to the popular, human palate rather than to that of the exquisite, the intellectual snob and the sophisticate. And let me remind today's thinner-blooded arbiters of taste that the greatest art which Japan ever created — and for well over a thousand years Japan has been a highly artistic and a highly sophisticated nation — occurred at a moment when it abandoned the courtly and scholarly idiom and stooped to the Yedo and the Yoshiwara.

Mass media, then, can render possible a more popular and democratic art, appealing to an ever-larger audience. There is another economic fact in contemporary life which may make such an art imperative. In 1940, well after the end of the depression, it occurred to me that it would be interesting, not only to establish the average annual income of our artists, but also to discover how much of this income was derived from the sale of easel paintings, how much from commissioned work — murals and portraits — and how much from such supplementary sources as teaching and writing. I therefore sent out questionnaires to a hundred of the most prominent, nationally known American artists, selecting the names of those painters who had appeared most frequently in the catalogues of our leading museums over a period of eight years. Every artist on my list had been invited to the Whitney Museum; almost all of them had been invited to the exhibitions of the Museum of Modern Art, the Corcoran, and the Chicago, San Francisco and Philadelphia annuals. Some of the artists were from Texas, Chicago, New Mexico and California; but the great majority were from New York or its vicinity and had business connections with Fifth Avenue and Fifty-seventh Street dealers. The work of most of them had been exhibited in Paris, London or Venice, and much of it was in the permanent collections of many of our museums. The average age of these artists was perhaps fifty. That is, they had reached their full maturity.

Of these artists only ten had earned over $3,000 a year from sales of their work. But if the four painters having incomes of over $5,000 were excluded, the average annual earnings of the rest would be $1,389! This, then, was the not altogether satisfactory answer to the financial hopes and ambitions of "18,087 art students attending the leading art schools throughout the country." The unusually successful and gifted — one out of each 180 — could look forward toward the age of fifty to an income from the sale of his work of less than $2,000. Many of these artists of course supplemented their income from other sources: from teaching, lecturing, and commissions from the federal government or from private sources. Taken together the average earned income from all sources was $3,719, almost twice as much as was received from the sales of the artists' noncommissioned work.

When it is remembered that since 1940 our nation has been engaged in two long wars and that today our taxes are geared to an annual Defense Budget in the neighborhood of forty billion dollars, it will not seem surprising that subsequent polls have substantiated the general trend of my findings. Our civilization — here and in Europe — must face the paradox that there is a greater demand and a greater need for art than ever before; and at the same time the artist is having increasing difficulty in selling his pictures. From now on, more and more art will be supported on the basis of services rendered rather than on the basis of sales on a speculative art market. This emphatically does not mean that the public will stop buying paintings, sculpture, and prints. It does mean that even the most publicized artists will derive a larger fraction of their income from earnings for a service rendered — private or government commissions, teaching, lecturing, and so forth.

"The outlook, however, for American artists is not entirely discouraging, if once they and the general public face the fact that the means of rationalizing art in this not altogether rational world is slowly changing. And I am convinced myself that the outlook for a vigorous flowering of American art, integrated and scaled to the hopes and tastes of countless millions of Americans, rather than to the pocketbooks of those who still continue to buy French Modernism on Fifty-Seventh Street, is still more hopeful. More and more in a world apparently tottering to self-annihilation on the logic of Nineteenth-Century scientific progress, the human mind is searching for the critical values which it has lost in its worship of Nineteenth-Century scientific materialism. More and more Americans seem to be discovering these values in art, which is and always will be the greatest critique of human behavior."

In these words I expressed my optimism and faith in an article in *Harper's Magazine* in September 1940. At that moment the New Deal Mural Program was still alive. The curiosity of American artists in their own country was still fresh. Their zest for the positive rather than the negative statement, their healthy appetite for the visual, sensuous world about them had not been destroyed by the deadening shock of two wars and by the state of emotional suspension which grips our throats today.

Today if Modern Art is to regain its vitality it must respond to the challenge of such catastrophic events. It must round out its mission as the organic expression of a living world.*

---

* "American art must prove to the mass of its own citizens its ability to help them to individual fulfillment" (Laski, in *American Democracy*).

19'

ART AND COMMUNICATION

From the Author's Diary, June 6, 1953. I have shown the manuscript of my book to two or three of my friends. One of the statements in it which to them seems debatable is my assertion that nonobjective art will never have as wide an audience as representational art. I was discussing this question the other day with Robert Beverly Hale, who is the most open-minded and objective man I know in his desire to give every expression of art its day in court.

"But how can you be sure," he asked, "that when we are conditioned to abstract, nonrepresentational painting, we shall not be moved by it exactly as we are moved by the abstract, nonrepresentational pattern in music? How do you know that when this occurs abstract art will not have as wide an audience as music?"

I said: "In the foreseeable future and as long as civilization and human nature remain what they now are, we never shall be so conditioned. Children will still instinctively continue to communicate in pictures their response to the visual experience of life. Men and women will continue to think of the graphic and plastic arts as a means of communication, just as they think of language as a means of communication."

I remember how forcibly I was struck by the answer of a Patroness of the Pennsylvania Academy of Fine Arts to the efforts of my old friend and teacher, Henry MacCarter, who, in 1913, was patiently attempting to hoist her up to the cultural level of 1870 in some sort of an understanding of French Impressionism.

"But you cannot make me believe," she answered him with the unruffled serenity of a mother talking to a wayward and obstinate child, "that a white tablecloth is green."

A white tablecloth may be painted every color of the rainbow, as long as the picture communicates the fact that it is a tablecloth.

There is nothing difficult to understand in such nonobjective painting as does not purport to convey an experience or represent an observed fact of the visual world. Since it has divorced itself of subject matter, fiction, the anecdotal and sentiment, it does not tell us in communicable language anything that can be apprehended by the mind or related to an experience. Either we like it or we don't. You don't understand spinach or the color of a sunset or the odor of a flower. It is a matter of enjoyment or distaste. It is a stimulus to a direct sensation to which we respond emotionally. It is only when abstract or nonobjective art *purports* to communicate — and does not — that the trouble begins.

In such cases there are two sorts of noncommunicability — the one in which the painting attempts to convey an idea but does so ineffectively; the other, in what artist or critic says about the painting. Ten years ago I wrote in the *Atlantic Monthly* that much current criticism was double-talk or a meaningless jargon and was largely responsible for confusing the general public in the meaning and purpose of Modern Art. More recently forty-seven distinguished American artists signed a statement in *Reality* that art theories are "presented by a dominant group of museum officials, dealers, and publicity men . . . in a ritual jargon equally incomprehensible to artist and layman." Let us look at the record.

Excerpt from *Art News,* November 1952: "Seymour Lipton (Parsons) is focussing on movement in tension as seen in biologic forms of seed and flower. His sculpture, bronze melted on steel and nickel silver, is a witness of the inside and outside process of change and unfoldment in time. *Night Bloom* is a pod bursting and as such it is quite simple and graphic, yet the stress in material creates a tension in which space is opened and yet strongly enclosed by a definite awareness of the formula of nature in which freedom is always arbitrated by law . . ."

Excerpt from the review of Jean Dubuffet in *Art News,* February 1952: "The shock of the impact of these disgusting paintings should have indicated what a fine artist he was . . . By throwing quality away, quality is what he attains."

Excerpt from the *Art Digest,* November 1, 1952: "Hans Hofmann . . . His dynamic *Nocturne* is an apogee of pure color, of passionate paint love. He builds plane upon plane, color upon color, until the skin of the painting, like the crust of the world, is pitted with grooves, troughs, rivulets, caves, cataracts. Color and texture embrace a universe of flesh, of members, of wombs, of secret heart chambers and viscera."

Over the years new painting techniques and graphic formulae emerge into the spotlight or are forgotten along Fifty-seventh Street. The reviewers on *Art News* and the *Arts* (formerly the *Art Digest*) warble on in the same turgid and rhapsodic style. L.C., in the *Art News* of January 1956, has this to say of William H. Littlefield: "His 'ambivalent figure-ground integrations' . . . are made by allowing paint to pour into ropy figures in turn enclosing other figures. He builds up some parts with sand and other textures. The effect is of something grand and ruined, a Victorian house with all its furnishings left without tenants." And in the Summer Number of the same year P.T. writes of Dusti Bougé: "Her natural freedom of stroke and 'organic' rectangles of color are modified dialectically by a sensitive though discontinuous webbing." Of Paul Dieu the same critic writes: "This French newcomer deals in spacious areas on which, in two cases, fastidiously drawn congeries are elaborated with spatter and drips; the architectonic effect is of magically animated maps or, as in the other two cases, a rain-drenched wall at night and a row of stark, monolithic, untranslatable ideograms."

Soaring from the arid wastes of art criticism into a purer atmosphere of devotional poetry Leo Steinberg whispers of Philip Guston's color, in the *Arts* of June 1956, "The blind, red windowless organic interiority gains self-awareness by virtue of the foreign body, the intruding gray. The gray pain, the gray hunger, twining with red-roaring guts, becomes the agent of awakening awareness — I am in pain, therefore I am.

"But . . . their last effect — when the initial shudder over these thick smears has passed — is a remote and radiant joy, the very quality in fact, which again and again tempts one to locate these worlds of entrails in the sky. In their slow, tempered breathing there is not a thread of conflict, and no violence. The intrusive grays are linked and latched to the organic fiber, the two sustain each other like a warp and weft; the grays, for all their otherness, become a necessary and a welcome presence, and the picture smiles with ashes in the mouth."

The above quotations are the carefully considered statements by critics and reviewers of our leading art magazines. A Maine farmer, who has little knowledge of esthetics but shrewd practical sense in his own stony fields, would call it hog-wash — or perhaps just bull. Which it is.

Moreover it is a conscious fraud: a fraud that does great injury to Modern Art, often to the artist who talks in this not too witty, not too modern nursery jargon.* Not that all art publications, critics, reviewers and artists are guilty of using this fraudulent and muddy balderdash. But I am talking here of those who purposely use an unintelligible mash with a conscious effort not to be understood.

The Modern Idiom has introduced many new elements of design; new symbols, intervals and dissonances, to which the ear of the layman is not yet attuned. Much spurious and imitative painting is also presented to the public along with the truly genuine and occasionally the truly great. Tradition and time — the "solvent of all things" — will eventually establish standards by which the public can itself exercise discrimination. Until then artist and critic should use patience, clarity, and above all honesty in presenting contemporary art to the public. Many intelligent laymen are only too eager to be informed about the new modes, new patterns and new techniques, which they dimly sense to have beauty and meaning. But they are not willing to swallow a lot of garbage, and to have critic and artist make monkeys of them.

Picasso is a painter of enormous dexterity and very great importance. *Art News* is no mushroom publication, no "little magazine." It caters to the big collectors and carries the advertisements of Duveen, Wildenstein and Paul Rosenberg. It is the mouthpiece of some of the most powerful and shrewdest art galleries and art cartels in the world. Its voice carries authority. Artists who are exhibited in our leading museums carry authority — not just in their paintings but in what they say about them. Often what the critics and the artists affirm about Modern Art is harder for the public to digest than the actual paintings.

Much disservice is being done to Modern Art by this sort of packaging. One proof of this is the ease with which for over a generation the public has assimilated Modern Design in the crafts — in furniture, book

* "My painting, *Owh! in San Pao,* like my *Amazene,* and *Rapt at Rappaports,* are statements in a visual-proprioceptive idiom as simple as a tabloid headline. Anyone with enough coordination to decipher a traffic beacon, granted they accept the premise of its function, can handle their communicative potential with ease. There are no mathematics of Abstract or Naturalist Expressionistic Idealism to befuddle here, and the Department of Philosophical Displacement Relativisms is on the floor below. Emotion and Feeling, that crucial Emulsion, is a dimension at right angle to the plane of the canvas in these paintings" (Stuart Davis, in *University of Illinois Exhibition of Contemporary American Painting,* 1952).

and magazine illustration, fabrics and industrial design. These have been presented without chicanery or double talk. Is this meaningless double talk in the interpretation and presentation of Modernism by their own protagonists the hangover of some early protest or a more recent symptom of our perplexed and disordered world?

Much of it is the residue of a somewhat elephantine and outmoded humor, which at the turn of the century and well on through World War I was in vogue among the Parisian intelligentsia, the aristocracy of Montmartre and the XIV Arrondissement. To clown was the essence of wit. Picasso has always been a past master at this sort of drollery.* He has drawn no little satisfaction from exhibiting some study in abstraction with a title which could completely throw the audience off the rail. It is again the jack-rabbit mentality: coax the bourgeoisie — the pack of howling imbeciles — down an indicated trail, and then by a deft back-track leap — and what is better than a misleading title — send them yapping up the wrong alley. Degas, speaking of Whistler, another artist addicted to the same questionable wit, once said: "To hear him speak, one would hardly suppose that he knew he was an artist." The little Picassos emulate the less convincing tricks of the Master.

Much of this compulsive drive not to be understood may come from a persistent sense of inferiority, which lingers on from the early years of the Modern Movement, when sincere and sensitive painters were sneered at and ridiculed by their own profession, as well as by the public at large. I remember back in Paris in 1925 visiting with a friend, a talented American painter, B., in his studio in the Rue de la Grande Chaumière. My friend asked B., quite seriously and politely, "What does this painting mean? I don't understand it." An angry gleam came into B.'s eye. He said: "It means 'Kiss my ass.' "

Much of the will not to be understood comes, however, from a far deeper neurosis. It is caused by the subconscious fear which grips our

---

* ". . . fandango of shivering owls souse of swords of evil-omened polyps scouring brush of hairs from priests' tonsures standing naked in the middle of the frying-pan — placed upon the ice cream cone of codfish fried in the scabs of his lead-ox heart — his mouth full of chinch-bug jelly of his words — sleighbells of the plate of snails braiding guts — little finger in erection neither grape nor fig — commedia dell'arte of poor weaving and dying of clouds — beauty cream from garbage wagon — rape of maids in tears and in snivels — on his shoulder the shroud stuffed with sausages and mouths . . ." (Pablo Picasso, in *Dreams and Lies of Franco*).

times and slowly gnaws at man's more normal and healthy instinct to be himself. It is only through fear that animals — and the minds of men as well — crawl deep into their caves, bury their heads in the sand or throw up an ink screen, like the frightened squid in his effort to muddy the waters.

There is another kind of noncommunication between artist and public — not the failure of what is said in words about a painting by a critic or the artist himself — but what the painter fails to put across in his attempt to communicate in the abstract or nonobjective idiom. In the great majority of cases the artist does not purposely try to mislead his audience. The abstracted symbols which have a clear meaning to him, however, lack the same universally clear meaning for others.

Those ages and civilizations which could not sense a plausible pattern in the pervading sorrow or enigmatic ruthlessness of the outer world have, as I have pointed out, sometimes turned their gaze inward in search of emotional relief and a spiritual oneness. Buddhism, early Christianity, Islamism, the Middle Ages, or the cultures of such primitive peoples as American Indians and African tribes, have all expressed this turning in upon themselves, this longing for self-revealed truth, by an introverted art, more or less abstracted in design and divorced from the representation of lived experience and the visual world. Such art may be highly expressive and noble, as long as a proper balance is retained between spirit and flesh, the mind and the eye, the inward and the outgoing gaze — as long as the artist and the age which he mirrors have not too far escaped from the realities of life.

This preoccupation with religious themes and the attempt to express universal concepts through symbols is characteristic of the abstract or semi-abstract work of many contemporary artists. I have in mind the paintings of Abraham Rattner, Rico Lebrun, Peppino Mangravite, Pat Trevigno, Samuel Rosenberg, Hyman Bloom, Samuel Adler and others. Nor is the work I speak of concerned with Biblical episodes, but with a deep spiritual and religious wonder and meditation.

Other artists, too, interpret their work as an effort to express the visual world in universal terms or symbols. One cannot help noting the difference between the avowals of these contemporary artists and the interests and preoccupations of the Impressionists and of painters of earlier periods. For the latter talked more readily about techniques — the problems of light, form, and design, the mastery of good drawing, and the manner in which the artist could best transcribe nature on his canvas.

Seymour Fogel speaks of the "wonders all about us . . . which are facets of an underlying, eternal truth." Charles Umlauf states his philosophy that "a genuine art should have spiritual content in the religious sense." "Representation is not the thing I work for," says Pat Trevigno. "It is the spirit I want." "What is painting, what is art?" asks Richard Ruben. And his even more explicit answer: "To me a religion, a philosophy, a way of life." Fritz Glarner speaks of his development as an artist through his "search for the establishment of essential values." Walter Quirt affirms, too, that he is "searching for ways to record experiences visually in such form that ideas behind experiences are made more important than the experiences." Max Beckmann has said: "What I want to show in my work is the idea which hides itself behind so-called reality." And Abraham Rattner sums up the vague pervading mysticism that haunts many artists today: "I believe a new era is already here, that an awakening has already taken place, that a new age will be marked by the imposition of the spirit on the materialism of tomorrow." * (See Fig. 21.)

How different was the note with George Bellows or Glackens or Luks or Henri a generation ago. Thomas Eakins had the conviction that American artists must create a *native* art, "peer . . . into the heart of American life";† and Paul Cézanne reiterated again and again that the painter must study the classics, but only to prepare him for a better understanding of nature. Degas, too — as also his pupil Mary Cassatt — had repeatedly affirmed his veneration for the cinquecento: "Il faut se plier devant les primitifs." And Corot had written: "Beauty in art is truth, bathed in an impression received from nature." And Leonardo, who could be said to have ushered in the Age of Science, stated his simple faith: "A good painter is to paint two things, namely man and the workings of a man's mind."

For these artists worked in the tradition of the Renaissance — humanism and a study of nature. To a greater or lesser degree certain phases

* The quotations from Fogel, Umlauf, Trevigno, Beckmann and Rattner are from Ralph Pearson's *The Modern Renaissance in American Art.* The quotations from Ruben, Glarner and Quirt are from *Contemporary American Painting, 1952,* issued by the University of Illinois Press.
† Van Wyck Brooks, in *The Confident Years.*

of Modern Art, and more especially Abstract and Nonobjective painting, have broken with this legacy.

I surely would not dissent with or call in question the widespread yearning of Modern Art to establish new values and concepts of life. Artists today have the solemn duty to set their bearings straight and readjust their criteria, to consider where they are going and the Why and What of their art. Just as Modern Design has contributed a new idiom of expression, so Modern Art has rejected the shop-worn realism of nineteenth-century materialism and is groping for a new expression of faith, which can better interpret the positive hopeful organic meaning, rather than the negative protest, of our age.*

But how successful have these extreme abstract and nonobjective artists been, notwithstanding their sincerity, in communicating their faiths and needs and yearnings? For most obviously the artists whom I have quoted would not be satisfied in creating an art of purely sensuous delight. And it is hardly possible for me to take seriously the professions of some of their group that their art is a vastly serious affirmation which they do not at all care to communicate to the world. This dilemma is not something to be laughed away. It is indeed a tragedy. For I believe that American art — apart from its technical dexterity, its tonal brilliance, and its rich texture — has a content which is of vast importance to our world, a content which is often frozen in the icy wall of noncommunication.

I believe that our nation has not entirely lost its traditional optimism, its closeness to the soil, its yes-saying, its forward-looking and forward-stepping and up-standing approach to life. I believe that American art has a future, and that this future is not just to tickle the jaded palates of hedonistic esthetes, but to assert in a modern idiom *which can be understood by all* the verities that are as old as is our nation, as old as the Hellenic-Hebraic tradition from which was born our Western World.

* "As I see the age in which I live, I think it is a very difficult and very confused age. And I think there are several patches in it which are laboring and sweating and striving to get towards a clarity — often in confused ways, but still laboring and sweating and I think these pictures are a part of that sweating and striving. I don't believe they are on the way down. I believe, on the whole, they are on the way up," writes Gregory Bateson, in *Modern Artists in America* (New York: Wittenborn, 1952).

20 ´

ART AND TRADITION

From the Author's Diary, April 26, 1950. I am painting a head of Raphael Soyer and he one of me. We are to exchange them. (See Fig. 34.)

There is something "old world" about this gentle and sincere man, his complete immersion in and passion for his art and his interest in his fellow artists.

We had just left Julio de Diego's studio, where Julio, Xavier Gonzalez, Sam Adler, Raphael, myself and others had been working on lithographs for the Equity Dance Catalog. We both had noted X's nervous excitement, amounting almost to rapture, as he slopped tusche up and down on a strip of cardboard. This he then transferred by pressing it down on a zinc plate in order to obtain a certain sensuous unpredictable texture, into which with two or three heavy strokes he rapidly drew what might — or might not — represent a human figure.

He was pleased with the result and said: "One never has enough courage in art. One should not be afraid to let oneself go."

Commenting on this later at lunch and speaking of the school which it represents, I said: "It is arts and crafts — good or bad — but it is not serious painting."

Raphael said: "It depresses me. Perhaps we are at the end of an epoch. Perhaps with photographs and the movies there is no need for the art of painting. The public may not want it. Arts can die. Like human beings or nations. The great art of painting may be finished forever."

Later while we were working he said: "At one moment in my life I thought I should be a writer. My father was a scholar. He wrote children's stories in Hebrew. But I deliberately chose painting as my career. I thought of painting then as dealing with human beings, the visual world, the drama of life. If I had known then that painting would take this direction, I might have chosen otherwise. But I shall keep on painting, as I do now, until I die. It is the thing I care most about in life. I cannot do otherwise."

He was very depressed. God knows, I am myself. Both of us feel — most of the finest artists of my generation, modern or traditional, feel — that the present moment is one of chaos, chicanery, and double-talk in the art world. There are no valid critical standards. Perhaps all this is a reflection of the chaos of

the world. Certainly Europe has lost her fine sense of critical tradition. As far
as painting goes, we never quite had one.

I said to Raphael: "I am less pessimistic than you about the future. All this
is a passing fad and a passing phase. The sort of art now in vogue has little
meaning and that little meaning has never been understood by the public at
large. How quickly water runs over the dam. You and I can remember when
the Ashcan School was the thing of the moment, and later Cubism and Mar-
cel Duchamp, and still later when Tom Craven was the impresario of the
Regionalism of Tom Benton, Steuart Curry, and Grant Wood. That was as
recently as 1939."

"What has happened to Tom Benton?" Raphael asked.

I said: "I hear that he is running for United States Senator from Missouri."

André Malraux, who is always provocative, if never quite profound,
has suggested in his *Psychologie de l'art* that artists are inspired and respond first and immediately to an inherited culture and only indirectly
to nature. For they can only see nature in terms of yesterday's art. His
fallacy lies of course in confusing the raw material and inspiration of
the artist, which is nature, with his inherited idiom of speech, which
is style. His whole thesis is indeed an amplification of Whistler's *bon mot*
that nature copies art, meaning simply that we see things in the style or
idiom in which we have been taught to see them. Malraux goes on to
say that through the new techniques of physical and visual communication — bodily access to the hidden treasures of the world, colored photography and the new methods of reproduction — a modern museum has
been created. This museum has given, and in the future increasingly will
give, to Modern Art a universal stamp which it could never have had
before; and it will be one of the dominant factors in molding the art of
the future. His whole thesis depends, then, on something which he takes
a little for granted, the force of tradition in Modern Art.

Modernism, like every great period, is eclectic in that it has refreshed
its heritage from many foreign sources of inspiration. But the great
weakness of the movement is, not just that in its eagerness for experimentation in new modes it has jettisoned the outmoded styles of the past, but
that it has thrown overboard, too, the very need of tradition. Those of
us who lived in the art world of Paris just before World War I remember
the vehemence with which the young Cubists and Futurists attacked the
"cult of the past, the obsession with the antique, the pedantry and for-

malism of the academies." * Now this rejection of tradition can be a very grave danger. For eclecticism without tradition results in chaos rather than style.

Nothing in life is ever quite new. The spring bud pushes itself up from last year's seed, and the taller the cedar tree, the deeper its tap root has thrust into the earth. Nor can one leap high in the air without taking off from solid ground.

I had the rare fortune in my first year as an art student in Paris to fall under the spell and influence of Mary Cassatt, the influence of an integrity and passion and a very masculine objectivity in a very prim and feminine exterior. She never confused art with bohemianism. She never confused her veneration for Degas as an artist with her contempt for him as a moral being. She never confused originality with the disavowal of tradition, or creative imagination with the rejection of discipline. As a very young woman she had been accepted as one of their own by the members of the most radical art movement of the century. As a very old woman she said to me in answer to my interrogation as to the wisdom of copying Rembrandt: "No. Rembrandt is *le dernier mot*. Go to Florence and study the *quattrocento*. You know what Degas said: 'Il faut se plier devant les primitifs.'"

For Europe — and Italy more than any country in Europe — has had that wealth of experience, that rich memory of the past, which in art as in human beings breeds maturity. And it is surely a disavowal of this sense of tradition, so characteristic of the Modern Movement, which prompted Brancusi's "Michel Ange, c'est du biftek!" and which inspired Umberto Boccioni, the young Italian Futurist and pamphleteer to publish his "peremptory conclusions to destroy the cult of the past." And

* "Here are our peremptory conclusions:
"To destroy the cult of the past, the obsession with the antique, the pedantry and formalism of the academies.
"To despise utterly every form of imitation.
"To extol every form of originality . . .
"To draw courage and pride from the facile reproach of madness, with which innovators are lashed and gagged.
"To rebel against the tyranny of the words 'harmony' and 'good taste.'
"To sweep from the field of art all motifs and subjects that have already been exploited.
"To render and glorify the life of today, unceasingly and violently transformed by victorious science" (Umberto Boccioni, an Italian Futurist painter, in *Artists on Art*).

this same disavowal of the weight of tradition is implicit in the recent manifesto of the group of American Post-Abstractionists that laid down as dogma the patent absurdity that with the Modern Movement "a purely abstract art came into being. During this period, painting has demonstrated that art lives by formal terms." * For Abstract Art is as old as the earliest art of which we have any record. And for that matter all art is formal, since without form there could be no art.

Six years ago, driving through Apulia in Southern Italy after a ten-hour trip across the Apennines, we put up at the Albergo Satti in Foggia. Marguerita Sarfatti, who was with us, asked the *portiere* from what province in Italy he came. He answered: "Sono di Mantua, il paese del poeta Virgilio."

Only an Italian could have said with such innocent simplicity that he was aware and not ashamed of his country's artistic tradition. All through European literature we run across charming instances of the honor and deference of great men to the great men who had preceded them, without whose earlier efforts they knew that they themselves could not have achieved greatness. Delacroix, who was himself an innovator and plowed the ground for Modernism, used to say to his students, of Ingres — with whom he fought all his life, but who represented the classic French tradition — "Messieurs, when you walk by his paintings, your hats in your hand, but your eyes on the ground."

I know of no more touching passage to express this reverence for greatness than Boswell's description of his encounter with the formidable Dr. Johnson on May 16, 1763, when Mr. Davies "having perceived him, through the glass door of the room in which we were sitting, advancing toward us, he announced his awful presence to me." One undoubted reason why Europeans of Boswell's generation had a clear and

---

* "Almost half a century has passed since a purely abstract art came into being. During this period, painting has demonstrated that art lives by formal terms. This exhibition [at the Provincetown Art Association, August 1950] gives proof of a new sense of painting that can be termed post-abstract. Post-abstract painting goes beyond formal relationship, it communicates plastically, sensually and psychologically through the inherent qualities of paint. It goes directly from the painter to the observer, without reference to the naturalistic world, creating an image of its own in a mysterious existence. The inventiveness and conceptual freedom explains the variety in use of the means of expression."

Among the signers of the manifesto were Richard Poussette-Dart, William A. Baziotes, Theodoros Stamos, David Hare, Adolph Gottlieb, Karl Knaths, Robert Motherwell, Jackson Pollock and Hans Hofmann. (See Figs. 23, 25, 26.)

vigorous style, was the respect they bore for the great craftsmen of their language.

In the winter of 1936–37, teaching art at the Colorado Springs Fine Arts Center, I often discussed with Boardman Robinson, who was a very great teacher, the apparent lack of interest among the students in those particular artists, American or European, for whom they showed some natural affinity. Too often the students seemed interested only in their own expression. Robinson and I speculated as to how much this very American weakness is the result of a pioneer background, which is ever casting off and leaving behind, under the impression that it actually creates new forms, when all it does is to transplant old ones into a new soil and climate. And years later during World War II, listening to our G.I.'s discussing world events among the limestone outcroppings of Sicily or Southern Italy, I would hear much the same comment: "I guess we can get along without Europe and her past."

At the Fine Arts Center I was a little shocked by the unwillingness of the trustees to acquire any paintings — even as gifts — which would establish something like a fixed standard, allowing the student to measure his advance or retreat, to fix his esthetic bearings, in the fluid modern field of line, color and design. "We must not interfere with the students' effort to find their own direction through the weight of tradition," they said. And often since then when some of our museums periodically decide to unload certain earlier schools of painting, it has been done on the assumption that the directors were only interested in contemporary trends of painting. But can such an exclusive interest in contemporary art ever have a truly fruitful and dynamic influence unless the current "stream of consciousness" is directly related to the many sources from which it flows?

The rejection of tradition can result not merely in a weakening of the reservoirs of creative strength upon which the artist must draw, but also in the loss of the techniques of a profession. As painter-member of the Commission of Fine Arts I was occasionally asked to recommend an artist of distinction to paint the portrait of some cabinet member or government official. A few years ago I wrote to the director of a leading American museum — one that prides itself on keeping in touch with the

27. José Clemente Orozco. *Prometheus.* Pomona College

28. George Biddle. *Cannibalism of War* (central panel). Mexico City

29. Joseph Young. *Mosaic.* Temple Emanuel, Beverly Hills

30. Stuart Davis. *Flying Carpet.* Wool rug. Museum of Modern Art

31. George Biddle. *Ceramic*

32. Georges Rouault. *We Think Ourselves Kings.* Museum of Modern Art

33. Ben Shahn. *The Violin Player.* Museum of Modern Art

34. George Biddle. *Raphael Soyer and His Model*

younger talent all over the country — and asked him if he could give me a list of half a dozen of the younger, less well-known but distinguished painters, capable of executing such a commission. I did not hear from him. Six months later I happened to run into him at an art gathering in New York.

He said to me: "I suppose you were surprised that I never answered your letter. But to tell the truth, I don't know any of the younger talented painters who could undertake such a commission. They don't seem to go in for portraits, and of course you know the older vintage as well as I do."

Yes; portrait painting as an art — rather than as a debased form of chromolithography — is very nearly a lost tradition.

In the spring of 1949 I was invited by the United Jewish Appeal to visit Israel. I was much impressed by the passionate fervor of the tiny one-year-old republic — emerging from the strain of a successful war with forty million adversaries — for the things of the spirit. Dr. Chaim Ganzu, the bushy-eyebrowed and loquacious little director of the Tel Aviv Museum, conducted me through the Galleries. In each gallery was exhibited that particular school of art which he felt had had an influence on Israeli painting. In one, the nineteenth-century schools of religious and romantic German, Austrian and Polish Jewish painters, in another French Impressionism, in still a third European Modernism. Coming to the large central gallery Dr. Ganzu said: "And here you see our contemporary Israeli art, derived from its many European sources." He was not primarily interested in Düsseldorf, Munich, or the Ecole de Paris; but very much so in the traditions from which Israeli art had grown.

Into our own traditions there flows, not just this vast European inheritance, but also our more immediate American background, which has formed our common speech. We can phrase our thoughts, of course, in a cosmopolitan tongue, but we tend to express the deepest truths of life only in our native idiom. For this local idiom is conditioned by our national mind and the human experiences that we have shared in our unique American approach to life.* The American temper and American

* Emerson was convinced that American Democracy "had an autochthonic quality about it which it owed, not to Europe, but to its own uniqueness" (Harold Laski, in *American Democracy*).

art have always had certain distinctive qualities. Generally they have been literal, romantic, and realistic, rather than theoretic or formal. In painting, our genius has shown a feeling for bold, simply stated design. We see this in John James Audubon's prints, in John Singleton Copley's early portraits, and in the works of our anonymous limners and primitives, such as Edward Hicks in his "Peaceable Kingdom," Joseph Pickett's "Manchester Valley," or the many beautiful lithographs of Currier and Ives.

At its narrowest and least important this local idiom is no more than "Regionalism." But it is well to remember that Chaucer wrote his *Canterbury Tales* in the common speech rather than in the language of the scholars and aristocracy of fourteenth-century England, and that Dante decided against composing the *Divine Comedy* in Latin. And it is equally true that Cervantes and Goya created universal works of art in a completely Spanish idiom. It is sometimes argued that there can be no *American art,* but only *art.* This statement, however, needs clarification. It is true that the artist probes for the essence of life. But he has only experienced the life that lies about him. And he finds his universal truth in his immediate and inherited surroundings. Never, never in a milieu or background with which he is unfamiliar. I do not believe that American artists today are consciously aping the Paris School. But how deeply are some of them aware that as Americans they can only give expression to universal concepts in their native speech?

"Where would our American railroads and ships and buildings and bridges and bathrooms be," asks Edmund Wilson in the *Triple Thinkers,* "if the techniques of engineering were taken as the arts and humanities are — so that students are graduated from colleges, and not merely from progressive colleges, and even take M.A. degrees, without having any idea of the top human achievements in their fields, without, often, being able to express themselves in decent English?"

The other day a very young student from one of our better-known liberal art schools asked me to criticize his paintings. They were all efforts in extreme abstract Expressionism.

I asked him: "Is drawing taught at your school?"

"Oh no. That is, not if we are interested in abstract art."

And the anatomy of design? And a survey of the different styles of design?"

He looked a little bewildered.

"I mean are you taught, for instance, the distinguishing elements and characteristics of Gothic and Renaissance design? Art nouveau? Mayan? Modern?"

"Oh no. We are encouraged from the start to express ourselves directly."

Perhaps the greatest tragedy in the general breakdown of tradition in the arts is the disregard for good drawing. For drawing is the rock and foundation, the ribs and skeleton, the basic framework of the visual arts. Good drawing has nothing to do with the reproduction of something seen. It is the painter's expressive language through visual symbols, rather than word symbols. And just as words, when properly used, have a life of their own, entirely apart from the objects in nature which they represent, so the drawn line carries the flavor and personality and breath of a great artist.

Yet in many of our art schools there is little or no emphasis on the basic need of sound drawing, and students graduate without the slightest proficiency; often unable to draw at all, and hiding their ineptness under the cloak of Expressionistic or nonobjective aspirations. Yet this ineptness, this lack of basic training, was in no way characteristic of the founders of Modern Art. Picasso is a great *dessinateur* — there is no appropriate word in the English language* — and Rouault, as a student and young artist, was a powerful academic draftsman. Matisse, too, in the school which he directed in the decade before World War I, insisted on his students' mastery in the life class. And Guillaume Apollinaire, the early friend of Picasso and the enthusiastic advocate of Cubism, wrote in his *Bestiaire*:

---

* It is one of those riddles of philology that in English there is no word for *dessinateur, Zeichner, dibujador, disegnatore,* etc. Even more curiously, considering the passion of the Latins for abstract thought, there is no separate word in French, Spanish, Italian, or Portuguese for "design." These languages content themselves to express this concept in the graphic arts with their word for "drawing" — *dessin, diseño, disegno,* etc. Sometimes I feel, however, that good drawing and good design are synonymous, the basic bone structure of the visual arts.

"Admirez l'artifice extrême
Et la beauté de la ligne."

This insistence on the nobility and subtlety and all-importance of the drawn line runs like a leitmotif through the history of Western art. Mary Cassatt had counseled me: "To study line, draw in drypoint or in silver point; for these media are the dryest, the most exacting and the least colorful. In them you are down to the bone. You cannot cheat."

Her master, Hilaire Germain Edgar Degas, with all the ill-tempered shabbiness which grew upon him with the years, showed only rectitude and probity in the practice of his art. At the age of seventy, speaking of the need of integrity in drawing, he said: "One must have an exalted idea, not of what one does, but of what one will some day accomplish."

Tintoretto had said: "Beautiful colors are for sale in the shops of the Rialto, but good drawing can only be fetched from the casket of the artist's talent with patient study and sleepless nights; and it is understood and practiced by few." *

And Titian, who was perhaps the greatest colorist who ever lived, had said: "It is not bright color but good drawing that makes figures beautiful." †

And Michelangelo, the poet of painters, had summed up his belief in the meaning of the line — what he felt was the beginning and the end of great art — when he and Pope Julius II stood under the vaulting of the Sistine Chapel. The Pope admired his craft and the nobility of his conceptions; the old painter replied: "It is a matter of good drawing. You can get the rest by pissing on it."

Edmond de Goncourt, in his life of Hokusai, one of the great draftsmen of all time, tells an anecdote of this foremost figure of the Ukiyoye school, who died in 1849 at the age of eighty-nine, leaving behind him over 30,000 drawings. On his death-bed the old man said: "I think if I were granted ten more years to live, I might learn how to draw." He fell back on his pillow. Raising himself again with an effort, he whispered: "Yes. Perhaps even with five more years I might learn how to draw." He then expired.

* From *Artists on Art.*
† *Ibid.*

ART AND GOVERNMENT

From the Author's Diary, Sunday, June 25, 1950. This morning over the radio it is announced that the Communists have invaded South Korea. Is this the beginning of World War III? Yes; unless the democracies act with vigor and haste . . .

Thursday, June 29, 1950. I waited for almost two hours and a half at the White House before I was admitted to keep my appointment with the President. He was standing beside his desk and I don't suppose I was with him for more than five minutes. We talked standing. He seemed vigorous and jolly. A little flushed. Shiny pink face. Perhaps overweight. He shook hands heartily and said: "Well, I guess you know you've been appointed to the Fine Arts Commission."

He talked about the Commission's work for a few moments. Said he had wanted to renovate it, that all bodies should be renovated every so often. That he wanted to enlarge the scope of its activities to include all the arts, such for instance as music.

I told him how happy I was that he was thinking along these lines. I mentioned very briefly the proposal of the Committee on Government and Art, representing all the art organizations of America, to ask him to name a commission to study the better integration of the cultural activities of the government. He said he felt the government could do more to use its cultural activities. He felt that the Fine Arts Commission could be expanded for such a purpose.

He laughed and said: "We're going to use you, but we have lots of fun down here in Washington."

I said: "I guess I'll have a lot of headaches; but if I can be useful to you, I'll be glad to help."

He said: "Francis knows me. I guess he's told you all about me."

I said: "I know what pressure you're under. These last few days you've been making history."

He laughed again. Pointing to the mass of papers on his desk, he said: "Well, we're making history all the time. You see I'm pretty busy. Sometimes the going is tough. But when things get cleaned up we'll have a talk about the whole situation."

I said: "I want to tell you one thing. You have no idea how many people have said to me these last few days — and I feel the same way — 'Thank God we've got a man in the White House who's got guts.'"

I think he was a little moved. We shook hands and I left.

At first blush it might be felt that the relation of Government and Art, although it may affect the economic security of the artist and, indubitably, the cultural life of the nation, yet has nothing to do with an analysis of Modernism or an inquiry into the creative process. Can a government copyright influence the chiseling of a sonnet? I think this point of view a little narrow and scholastic. If I am deeply concerned with Modern Art it is surely not as an abstract but as a living problem. If I have faith in the future of American painting, I look forward to a less inverted expression, a greater robustness and fertility, a wider communication and a fuller enjoyment. Now all these qualities directly depend upon the artist's audience. Therefore to a great degree they depend upon the artist's patronage. The government's deep concern in the creative life of the nation is part of the general background which affects the creative product of the artist.

The new concept of art as a social service with an educational value is perhaps as important a factor in its healthy development as the new idiom of expression, which is Modern Design. The Mexican murals and the New Deal Art Projects were significant achievements because the best of them combined the new idiom with the new social concept of art.*

My thinking toward the proper relation of Government and Art was of course deeply conditioned by talks and correspondence in this country with Roosevelt, Hopkins, Bruce and Cahill; and with José Vasconcelos,

---

* "With the loss of his standing as a craftsman, with the loss of standards of craftsmanship, the artist has become a kind of special being, a mysterious 'creator' encouraged to think of himself as unusual in every way. Some have become inverted and uncommunicative in the process, others have studiously cultivated unintelligibility. In either case the results are bad in that they have deprived the artist of an audience. Some means must be found to bridge the tremendous gap that has grown up between the painter and the public, some midway point at which the creative person and the literate spectator can meet. Within the past twenty-five years the Western Hemisphere has seen two significant experiments in that direction: the Mexican Renaissance and the government-sponsored art activities in the United States . . . " (Bernard Myers, in *Modern Art in the Making*).

Rivera and Orozco in Mexico. The particular tradition and sagacity of each country had a very direct bearing on its achievement. The outstanding genius of Mexico was the Latin respect for the freedom of expression of the artist. Mediterranean peoples are not congenitally afraid of ideas as such. They do not have a compulsive drive to correct, improve, whittle down and censor, to reduce intuition and imagination to conformism and mediocrity.

In 1942 I was invited with Hélène Sardeau by the Brazilian government to decorate with frescoes and mural bas-reliefs the National Library of Rio de Janeiro. I dreaded the thought of bureaucratic interference, which had weighed on me like a nightmare seven years before while I was working on a similar commission for our government. I therefore suggested to Gustavo Capanema, the Brazilian Secretary of Education, that I would prefer submitting my sketches for the approval of my friend Candido Portinari, who at that time stood high in the graces of government circles. Capanema looked at me a little dazed. "But I don't understand," he said. "As the artist you are the one who is responsible for the execution of the murals. Why should you have to submit the sketches to anyone? It is your job, although of course I should like to see them."

Hand in hand with this toleration for the artist's creative expression is the Latin's belief — amounting almost to passion — in the individual. It is foreign to his nature to "staff write" an editorial. It is foreign to his nature to work through committees, organizations, or juries. His impulse is to do the selecting himself. This is why Mexico has chosen many mediocre artists. It has also commissioned its greatest. This is why Mexican muralists have executed some third-rate murals. They have also painted the most significant murals since the High Renaissance in Italy.

The genius of America, the wisdom of Roosevelt and Hopkins and Bruce and Cahill, underscored another truth: that the only way to escape from the domination of vested interests, whether of political lobbies crusading for one-hundred-percentism and native sons or artists' pressure groups crusading for themselves — and the only impartial method for continually unearthing new and untried talent — is through open competitions, juried by qualified experts. The objective was to establish a technique of selection which would ensure a steady flow of creative excellence, after the Bruces, the Cahills, the Vasconcelos, and the Cap-anemas would be "out" with the next administration. As a result, op-pressed as it was with the American compulsive drive to correct, im-prove, whittle down, expunge and censor, the New Deal never got the very best out of its greatest artists. But owing to its technique of selection by jury it obtained a greater number of fine murals by outstanding artists and unearthed and used more young talent, in a shorter time, scattered over a wider range of territory, and at less drain of the taxpayer's money than ever before in our history.

The New Deal Art Projects were on the whole as humane, demo-cratic and intelligent as any art program the world over. By and large they had developed through trial and error. They were no brain-trust fantasy, but were suited to our needs, our tradition and our tempera-ment.

During these years there emerged and crystallized for me one or two ideas which would be my guiding stars and would orient for me any subsequent discussion of a government-sponsored art program.

The selection of artists for important commissions must be made di-rectly on the basis of past accomplishment — as in Mexico — never through juried competitions. For juried competitions by definition are the expression of a compromise, a norm, an average, never the extreme, never the worst, and therefore almost never the best. For the best is ex-treme by nature. Anyone who has served on a jury knows this. The jury system is a wise and necessary political compromise.

But there must always be in the vast majority of cases just such open, anonymous and juried competitions: because our country is vast, de-centralized and democratic; because human beings are not infallible, and what one man thinks is the best may turn out to be not so good; because the search for and try-out of new talent may be as important to our coun-try tomorrow as the promotion of acknowledged talent is today. In either case, whether the selection of the artist is on the basis of his past perform-ance or whether it is by open anonymous competition, the choice must be freely made — not subject to duress or arbitrary review — *by qualified experts*. This condition must be the artist's Bill of Rights in his future relations with our government.

And lastly let us with prayers and humility bear in mind that if there is such a thing as original sin, our own American legacy which the Devil planted in us is our intolerance of ideas, our lack of respect and reverence — not just for art — but for the other man's Yes and No. When we commission an artist on the supposition that he is the best man for the job, let us lean over backwards not to correct, improve, whittle, censor and strait-jacket him. Perhaps then he will give us his best. Once in a while even a masterpiece.

The Depression was the immediate, energizing cause of the New Deal Art Projects. America's dominant position in an unstable world is the immediate cause of our government's forthcoming sponsorship of the Fine Arts.

Little by little during the past decade the need of a vigorous, well-rounded, intelligent foreign cultural program had become more and more apparent to our State Department, to Congress, and to the various art organizations throughout the country. In 1949 Secretary of State Acheson had written me an expression of our government's policy to take with me to Israel, when I went there to co-sponsor the exhibition of paintings donated by our artists to the Tel Aviv Museum. "The arts, in which the universal voice of mankind finds expression, have always been one of the surest keys to understanding among civilized peoples." The policy of the State Department, Mr. Acheson continued, in furthering cultural exchanges with many countries is predicated on "the belief that the mutual understanding which they promote contributes to the friendly settlement of differences in a changing world . . . This program is closely related to the central purpose of the United States today in all its international relations, which is to join with other free peoples in bringing about a world where men may live with dignity and with faith in the future."

Secretary of Labor Tobin had proposed the creation of a Bureau of Fine Arts in the belief that our federal government "should seriously consider what can be done to further the arts in our country." Congressmen had introduced bills for the creation of a national theater and opera. Americans for Democratic Action, a liberal political, non-party pressure group, on whose Art Committee I had been active, had demanded in its 1950 platform that the President appoint a commission to explore the most effective means of "coördinating the Federal Government's present cultural activities."

Under the Chairmanship of Lloyd Goodrich, Associate Director of the Whitney Museum of American Art, the Committee on Government and Art, of which I was also a member, had passed a similar resolution during the winter of 1949, urging the study by a presidential commission of existing governmental cultural agencies. The weight of this committee would carry great authority, representing as it did every important art organization of America: the museums, the artists and the five hundred organizations and institutions affiliated with the American Federation of Arts.

Such was the pervading realization throughout government circles and the art world when in June 1950 war broke out in Korea, and that same week I was appointed painter member to the Commission of Fine Arts. It immediately struck me that chance had created circumstances through which the President might be approached and persuaded to appoint just such an impartial, qualified commission to study the current art activities of the government, to make recommendations for their more effective integration, and to advocate a more vigorous implementation of our foreign policy through an expansion of cultural relations with other nations. In a national emergency the chief executive of our country could hardly afford to waste much sleep on the creation of a Bureau of Fine Arts. He would be deeply concerned with any program which fitted into the picture of national defense.

On July 29, 1950, I wrote to President Truman suggesting that "unless the present war in Korea is localized, you may think it advisable, as in the last war, to mobilize the cultural forces of the country as part of an all-out effort. It is possible that you may feel the Fine Arts Commission might be the proper mechanism for such a program . . ." On August 3 he answered me: "I appreciated very much your letter of July twenty-ninth and I think your suggestions are good. We will look into the situation and see what we can do about it." The stage was set.

It had been my hope that the President might appoint a commission of outstanding Americans in every field of the arts, which could make a comprehensive report on the government's cultural activities. In a subsequent letter to me, however, he suggested that the matter might be properly discussed at the next meeting with the Commission of Fine Arts. He wrote me: "I understand that the whole Fine Arts Commission will be in to see me, on the twenty-fifth of January, and I will be glad to have a conversation with you on any subject you care to talk to me about at that time."

I drafted the following memorandum for the President. With a few alterations this was approved by the other members of the Commission on January 24, 1951, and the next day at our meeting with the President I presented it to him.

MR. PRESIDENT:

In the national emergency which our country faces — and will continue to face for the foreseeable future — you have indicated to me that you will feel the desirability of mobilizing the cultural activities of the Government, as of the entire country, in the overall picture of our national defense.

At present these governmental art activities are scattered, actually among ten different departments or agencies. The power which they could exercise both here and abroad is reduced and frittered. The State Department is aware of this situation and would welcome a greater use of art in our national education and to sell democracy to the world. The Defense Department, too, is without any effective program for the use of artists in making a historical record of our fighting troops; and in the use of camouflage.

There are existing agencies, however, which might be expanded to fulfill these and other cultural needs; immediately and without the necessity for congressional action. One is the National Gallery of Art and other cultural governmental institutions. Another is the American Federation of Arts, with over 500 affiliated chapters throughout the country. A third is the Commission of Fine Arts, which you know all about.

In England during the late war the Arts Council and the British Council were set up as emergency agencies. They proved so effective that they have been retained. Government subsidies are administered by civilian professional authorities. The Arts Council is an agency for the internal dissemination of art throughout the country. (Briefly what might be done by the Federation of Arts and also by an effective mural program under the Public Buildings Service.) The British Council disseminates art in the nation's foreign relations. (Briefly what the State Department needs to implement its foreign policies.) These two agencies offer today perhaps the most liberal, enlightened and effective art policy in the world.

The Commission of Fine Arts, Mr. President, is competent to investigate and make a report to you on the more effective integration of governmental cultural activities. It would have at its disposal the experience of the English

set-up, of the Office of the Co-ordinator of Inter-American Affairs of World
War II; of the War Department Art Committee of World War II; and of the
former art program under the Public Buildings Administration. In a minimum
time the Commission could give you practical recommendations on how best
to integrate and reorganize the present governmental art activities, in the
overall picture of national defense.

The following day the President requested the Commission to con-
duct a survey and to submit recommendations as to how such activities
could be more effectively coördinated or further expanded, under normal
conditions as well as during periods of emergency induced by war. For
nearly two years and a half the Commission worked on this report. The
members heard the testimony and suggestions of the Committee on Government and Art, of the State Department and of every other governmental agency engaged in cultural activities. The final report included
a lengthy summary of these activities and recommendations for their
better integration and expansion.

All the members of the Commission were united in the belief that
under our decentralized, diversified, federated, democratic tradition, it
would not be wise to follow the example of the highly centralized, gov-
ernmentally controlled and therefore bureaucratic Ministries of Fine
Arts, which since the seventeenth century have created the pattern of
government art patronage in most European countries. One of the unique
features of American culture is the diversification and cross-fertilization
of the many private groups and organizations which have sprung up from
coast to coast during the past century. In the field of the fine arts one has
in mind the city orchestras and museums, the local state and city art commissions, the Federation of Fine Arts with its five hundred affiliations,
the artist organizations, the college art centers, the endowments and the
art clubs, all of which are active in the promotion of the fine arts. The
geographical decentralization and local autonomy encourage a diversity
of style, private initiative and individual expression which make for
vigorous creative art. A centralized, bureaucratic control in our huge
and highly urbanized civilization would be stifling.

The vitality of our art is, then, in the long run dependent on the
initiative of private organizations and individuals—not on federal su-

pervision and federal subsidy. But our government can play a constructive role in stimulating the arts by coördinating and improving the cultural activities inevitably forced upon it; and by exploring the conditions which encourage the full and spontaneous expression of our creative citizens.

Federal sponsorship of the Fine Arts need not be in the nature of a relief agency, as was the Federal Art Project under the New Deal. It need not necessarily subsidize art any more than the Department of Labor subsidizes labor. It must concern itself with the needs and interest of the artist, just as the Department of Labor concerns itself with the problems of labor.

America is, however, almost the only great nation of the world today without a Ministry of Fine Arts and a clearly defined policy in its cultural activities. In the growing position of leadership in world events which we are forced to assume, it becomes daily more evident that we must make a more effective use of our cultural resources, in order to obtain and retain the respect of foreign nations. The spiritual and creative life of the nation, as much as its economic and physical health, must remain the deep concern of our government.

All of us on the Commission were in full agreement as to the danger of any centralized control, which might stamp a bureaucratic pattern on art bought or commissioned by the government. All of us recognized that there is no way by which one can perpetuate intelligent control by legislative fiat. In final analysis the success of any program will depend on the intelligence and ability of the persons directing it.

I felt, however, that in the design and decoration of federal buildings some technique must be established whereby the selection of artists and the supervision of their performance is wholly in the hands of a body of competent civilian experts — architects, artists, museum directors, or other qualified persons. Too often in the present set-up the selection of artists and the direction of art activities is either haphazard or politically controlled. It is sad to reflect that in such countries as Mexico and Brazil the outstanding creative artists of the country are employed to design and decorate public buildings. In the United States, with the exception of the work done under the New Deal Section of Painting and Sculpture, the over-all policies and the technique of selection too often result in an adequate academic performance, but almost never in outstanding creative work.

On this point — the reorganization and enlargement of the Commission in order to ensure such objectives — the other members of the Commission differed with me. They believed that the negative danger of government bureaucracy — incident in any attempt to control an intelligent selection of artists and the formation of a bold and progressive art policy — outweighed the positive advantages of such an effort. The difference in our approach to the problem seemed fundamentally to rest on a philosophy of optimism or complete pessimism as to the practical possibility of ever establishing in a democratic government an effective and liberal art program.

Whether the set-up which I suggested is practical or not; whether it is the best possible one, is largely a question of personal opinion, and perhaps can only be finally adjudicated by trial and error. It is surely a matter of general interest and should be open to discussion by those who are concerned with the future of art in America and the necessary part which our government will be forced to play in the picture. I believe that the government could accomplish much — as it did under the New Deal — to restore a healthy balance between the artist and his audience, to "bridge the tremendous gap that has grown up between the painter and the public," to change him from his position of isolation to a socially useful being. And I believe that this changed relation between the artist and the public might be the "impulse of some source of unseen power" to his creative expression.

MY OWN CREDO

I think that artists ought to recognize this, that there is no moral reason why art ought to go on if it has nothing further to express . . . Art is important only if it essays to be important. . . . Society needs more than anything else to be reminded that man is, in himself, ultimate value.

— Ben Shahn

Throughout these pages I have stated, implicitly or as a passionate conviction, a truth, which to me is absolute, for all ages and for all categories of art. It is that art concerns itself with life. Indeed in the most profoundly philosophic sense creative art is merely the most intense form of living. One complement of this truth is that painting, which is the visual art, must concern itself with the visual world, or it will become disembodied, a desiccated chrysalis, without living, breathing vitals. Another complement of this truth is that great art is that which concerns itself with the deepest, the noblest, the simplest, the everlasting qualities of human beings. That is the reason why great art will always be loved and understood by many millions of people for another thousand thousand years. Human character, human passions, human loves and hates have not changed much — as far as we can tell — in the last millennium.

At all seasons, all over the world, in every nation and race, human beings are born with certain particular inclinations and talents. They have natural, ingrained, personal aptitudes for visual expression, for word expression, for mechanical or scientific work, for social relations, business, or politics. They are born with natural rhythms in the ear or in the throat or in their bones and muscles, with natural coördination between eye and hand, which will predestine them to preëminence as

poets, musicians, dancers, or athletes. As far as it is known, these aptitudes are distributed, and always have been distributed, in relative, fixed
proportion among all people. God scatters his seeds — or his curses —
impartially.

For the present the point is this: Today in America, as in Paris at
the turn of the century, as in Athens in the days of Pericles, there is
born the same constant proportion of the population with a natural aptitude for art, for creating and enjoying painting, sculpture, and the
crafts. If this creative expression, this potential gift of appreciation is frustrated, it is because there is something in our contemporary education,
or civilization, that has smothered, frightened, thwarted one of the loveliest and most requiting and most valuable appetites in life. As George
Santayana says: "To feel beauty is a better thing than to understand
how we came to feel it. To have imagination and taste, to love the best,
to be carried by the contemplation of nature to a vivid faith in the ideal,
all this is more, a great deal more, than any science can be . . . Reflection is indeed a part of life, but the last part . . . The greatest pleasure
which we actually get from reflection is borrowed from the experience
on which we reflect."

Today in America this normal, healthy, human appetite for the enjoyment of art is being frustrated. It is being frustrated by the snobbism
of some of our museum directors and art critics, who are a little bewildered and afraid that they are not *le dernier chic; le dernier mot.* It is
frustrated by the misgivings of the common man — who, if he would
trust his better judgment, is so often right — believing that his taste is
low-brow and uneducated; and sometimes, alas, by the misgivings of the
artist himself, that he is "left at the post," an "also ran." It is being frustrated by the high-pressure salesmanship of some of our not-too-happy
New York art dealers, who with some of our not-too-happy museum directors set the fashion in the art world all over America. One of these
dealers recently said to me: "I am no longer young. I have done my bit
for American art. I must think of myself, and my wife, too. As long as
the collectors seem to prefer third-rate European nonobjective art to
healthy young American painting, why frankly I would rather sell it to
them." A museum director recently said to me: "I think they know bet-

ter. But who am I to stick my neck out." The normal healthy appetite of the public is being frustrated by the occasional double-talk, the sloppy thinking, the mumbo-jumbo of some of the art critics, who prefer to talk down their noses in a court language, on a plane way above the head of the ordinary little guy; and by a few of our artists, who keep rubbing in the fact — don't you believe them for a moment — that they don't need an audience and don't want to be understood.

But what is far more dangerous — because it depends not upon some fashionable and fleeting trend of the day but upon the suspension of a vital impulse of life — is the fear to face realities through an effort of the will; a fear which reflects the uncertainty of the world's long twilight time of troubles. It is the fear of looking with unflinching eyes upon the Yes and the No of life; the fear which raised Simeon Stylites to his small platform on a high pillar, where he could suspend himself above the actualities of the world below. It is the same fear which compelled a young and sensitive art lover to say to me last winter: "The world is too horrible. I want to get away from it. That is the reason why I prefer non-objective art. It offers an escape."

Emphatically I do not mean that the answer to this paralyzing fear is propaganda in art — the storytelling in paint of all the qualities and conditions which we believe make up the happy life. This is exactly what Soviet artists are compelled to paint. And this enforced service to the professions of a party, or of a faith, is what has stultified art in the totalitarian states.

Emphatically I do not mean that the controlling forces — the museum directors, the art critics, and the dealers — should brush aside, dismiss, relegate to the doghouse any form of expression or any sincere experimentation with the techniques of art, as they have relegated to the dog-house all art directly dealing with the visual world, with lived realities, with human values — in other words, all art which is understandable and satisfies the appetite of the ordinary man. That indeed would be jumping from the frying pan into the fire.

It is, however, a little hard for me to believe that the appetite of our young American painters and sculptors is confined to a series of abstract images and expressionistic symbols. I believe that many of these young painters and sculptors have other healthy appetites too. For human flesh and human forms and human faces. For the beckoning forms and articulation of animals, wild and tame — sometimes graceful, sometimes comic, sometimes fierce and strong. For the changing colors of the seasons — opalescent and pastel shades, full-toned reds and blacks and whites. For the changing shape and outline and color of our bold and varied land. For the odd and unimportant things that stand about the home — what John Millington Synge called "the profound and common interests of life."

Would not an occasional indulgence in such appetites add marrow and bones and fiber to our art?

I am convinced that into all this rich material, this human experience, our artists could weave the abstract patterns, the subtle or insistent color harmonies and the rich textures which now they so often see only through closed eyes in the dark recesses of the subconscious. For there is no question that our young painters are sensitive and skilled. And the integration of the visual world and human experience with their personal and Modern Design would offer a far more exciting challenge to their creative skill and imagination. On the whole it is far too easy to paint abstract pictures. Far too easy to understand them. It was Robert Frost who said: "For my own pleasure I had as soon write free verse as play tennis with the net down."

Once in Paris, sitting at the Dôme, I said to Ossip Zadkine about some mutual acquaintance: "He is not sincere." The little man smiled: "You are mistaken. All artists are sincere. It is a question of intelligence, imagination."

Yes. Most American artists are sincere. Many are talented. Many have imagination. And this escape from reality and the visual world is the creeping, paralyzing numbness, the fear which prevents so many of us from responding — not just to Buchenwald — but to life.

Paralysis and fear are not in the American tradition. As a nation we have often blundered. Expressed ourselves crudely too. At times our mountains have given birth to mice. But we have not often been afraid of life. So I do not believe this present escape in our art from life is a permanent trend. Fundamentally it is not an art problem but an American problem.

About twenty years ago when the ugly smell of Hitler's anti-Semitism had crept over the Atlantic and to some degree polluted and envenomed that always unstable element of the body politic which is subject to such infection, Jewish friends of mine would come to me with their fears — their fears about their position and future in America, caused by this world crisis, a crisis also whipped up and built upon fear. They spoke of their concern as the Jewish Problem. I, too, was disturbed. One day I talked about it to a wise friend of mine, Stanley M. Isaacs, then President of the Borough of Manhattan. He said: "There is no Jewish problem. There is an American problem. Always democracy will be under attack from recurrent hostile influences — germs or disease — trying to undermine the healthy organism. Our problem is to keep democracy sufficiently strong so that it will throw off the virus."

Thinking along the same lines I would suggest that perhaps there is no art problem with us today, but an American problem. There exists a universal world fear. In many countries the fear has taken different shapes. Many wise people believe that one of the masks which fear has put on is an escape from life. I believe that this escape from life draws the life blood from a vigorous art expression, as also from a normal appetite for healthy art. But the answer is not to condemn, or to attack, or to oppose escapist art. For escapist art may well be the expression of sincere artists. And one cannot stifle a sincere expression. At best one regrets it. The answer to escapist art is to banish fear.

During the two years that I spent in a Polynesian village I was impressed with the oneness of their ritual of art and life. Much of their art tradition had been broken down and bastardized by the impact of the missionary influence and Western civilization. Their music had remained very pure. When the men went on long trips into the mountains to gather the heavy clusters of mountain plaintain — *fei* — they would stop ever so often to rest. While resting, and sometimes weaving garlands of sweet-smelling fern, which they wore as easily as we carry a sprig of green in the lapel of our coats, they would improvise songs: short, simple lyrics, describing the beauty of the mountains, the palm trees, or the sea. Sometimes half in jest they would phrase a tribute to the strength or dexterity of a friend. There were other more time-honored district songs, short odes dedicated to their villages or to place names, which had acquired some family or tribal veneration. These odes were called *paripari*. There was one *paripari* about our village, Tautira. The words must have been very ancient because the song spoke of the *arioi*, the noble minstrels, whom Cook and Moerenhout speak of as having roamed the islands two hundred years ago. I made and kept a translation:

Moemoe fenua i Tautira e;	Tautira, land of revery;
O te torea iti apatoa e,	It is the little sandpiper from the South
I te ara mau ra e.	Winging down the true path.
O te taha iti i Vairua e.	It is Vairua's narrow strand.
O te ara iti otuitui e.	The little path, trembling to the pulse of the sea.
Tei Parirerire au e.	I am at Parirerire.
Ua mo'e outou i te arioi?	Have you forgotten the noble minstrels?
Tei hea te ara i Tautira nei?	O where is the path that leads to Tautira?

At night the youth of Tautira would often gather in the moonlight. Seated in a circle, one after the other, they would improvise short, erotic, and highly salacious couplets — *ute* — about each other. The music was fast and gay. The *ute* and the moonlight dancing were frowned on by the village elders.

But the finest singing was in the *himene,* the religious choral gatherings, held in the small frame houses of the church deacons. On religious or ceremonial days they were given in the pink-walled church. Natives came from many distant villages and camped with their friends or relatives. They sang all night, beginning about sundown. Every few hours they would refresh themselves with tea boiled in empty kerosene cans and loaves of bread baked at the store of Afa the Chinaman. The women sat cross-legged in the front rows, dressed in their long black Mother Hubbards. On a chair in their midst sat the *marutete,* the coloratura soprano, who improvised and wove her melody, in counterpoint, into the chorus. Behind was the bass accompaniment of the male voices. I fancy there were many quarter-tone intervals; and certainly no modes that I had ever heard. The singing produced a strange effect on me. The galloping rhythm, ever faster and more insistent, seemed to shake one's foundations — inside and out. Have you heard the cicada's late summer chant? And you cannot tell whether it comes from the sky or the trees or the ground under your feet, or whether it is one vibrating voice or ten thousand.

The villagers used to tell me — it sounds incredible — that the voices and the choral effects did not become harmonious — *mea navenave* — until they had been singing for six or more hours, well on into the dawn.

It is difficult to render in English the connotation of *navenave*, which I translate as harmonious. Tahitians use it to describe the supreme moment of sexual love, as also music which is completely satisfying. The only word I know which approximates its meaning is the French word *jouir*. I cannot help loving a people who instinctively have found the right word in which they pay tribute to the enjoyment of their native ritual art. An art form in which the entire community participates.

In our unique, federated, decentralized, democratic way of life, there is the deepest need for variety and experimentation. Our American civilization has always had a fluid pattern and we live in a fluid — a molten — world.

"We know that the safety of our civilization lies in making freedom of thought and freedom of speech vital, vivid features of our life . . . Our proudest boast has been a system that makes belief in the unorthodox a permissible way of life . . . Ideas, like the people who have them, need expression. The market place tests them — accepting a few, rejecting many. It is the interchange of ideas, the exploration of problems to their periphery, the challenge to prejudices that give any people the resiliency to meet changing conditions . . . There must be no limit on the range of temperate discussion, no limits on thought. No subject must be taboo. No censor must preside at our assemblies . . . We can never succeed if we limit ourselves to one creed, to one hypothesis, to one doctrine."

In these wise and manly words Justice William O. Douglas spoke his creed on the need of freedom of thought and freedom of expression for Americans today.* In turbulent periods of upheaval and change, flexibility and experimentation are needed for survival. They are the

* From the Lauterbach Award Address, New York City, December 3, 1952.

footings and foundations for a healthy art. In our painting there must be room for every expression and every school: for the Academicians, the Middle-of-the-Roaders, the Abstract and the Nonobjective, the Traditional — yes — even for the Lunatic Fringe. Meretricious art will never long survive, while the censorship of what we think is bad may strangle genius.

But healthy discussion will fertilize men's minds and the artist should make known his standards, his preferences and his faith.

I personally want an American art that deeply moves me. We are perhaps the most powerful nation in the world today. We are passing through one of the great crises in human history. Can we ask less of American art than something worthy of our destiny? Don't let us fool ourselves with the cowardly triviality — so often imputed to us from abroad — that the American genius does not express itself in art — that our contribution to civilization is in electric egg-beaters. I think of Emerson, of Thoreau, of Melville, of Walt Whitman, of Thomas Wolfe. I think of Frank Lloyd Wright. I have in mind our Negro spirituals, which only America could produce. I have in mind the portraits of John Singleton Copley and of Thomas Eakins, and the moonlight imagery of Albert Ryder. That is what I ask of American painting, and I believe that some of it is being produced in America today.

Yet to a great extent during the past fifty years — a period which will always be memorable in the history of art — the painter and critic alike have forgotten that, no matter in what medium the artist speaks, *life always has been and always will be the raw material of art.* Good painting — line, color and design — is never enough. One can enjoy the sensuous refinement of the artist's craft, but it is what he has to say with line, color and design that gives the ultimate significance to his painting.

Each artist, no matter how insignificant his contribution, will have some slightly fresh, new and individual approach to life. This indeed is the greatest contribution of art to civilization: that intuition of the nature of reality, distinct from reason and of equal importance, which justifies us in regarding art as an indispensable mode of knowledge.

The artist sometimes is unaware of the essence of his own intuitive outlook on life, on the nature and importance of his own contribution.

In a certain sense, this must always be the case. For a work of art, once created, has a separate life of its own. It grows or shrinks in stature as it sparks men's ideas or ceases to influence successive waves of human thought. But at other times, when in their lives nations feel the need of art, when art is needed by society and so becomes mature, the painter understands or thinks that he understands the ulterior, critical and prophetic meaning of his work: the intuitive reality which lies behind the conscious image of the visual world.

INDEX